W9-BRO-371

Honest
Answers

Jewish
Questions

✦ ✦ ✦

Honest Answers

TO YOUR CHILD'S

Jewish Questions

✦

A RABBI'S INSIGHTS

✦ ✦ ✦

Sharon G. Forman

URJ PRESS ✦ NEW YORK

For my children, Abigail, Joshua, and Benjamin, and all
of the children I have taught and from whom I have learned.

For permission to reprint, please contact the URJ Press at:

URJ Press
633 Third Avenue
New York, NY 10017-6778

(212) 650-4124
press@urj.org

Library of Congress Cataloging-in-Publication Data

Forman, Sharon G.
    Honest Answers to your child's Jewish questions: a rabbi's insights / Sharon G.
    Forman.
      p. cm.
    ISBN 0-8074-0944-8 (alk. paper)
      1. Judaism—Miscellanea.   2. Reform Judaism.   I. Title.

BM197.F67 2006
296—dc22   2006040443

This book is printed on acid-free paper.
Copyright © 2006 by Sharon G. Forman
Manufactured in the United States of America
10   9   8   7   6   5   4   3   2   1

Contents

Contents

Contents

Preface

When one guides sons and daughters in the right path, Scripture says, "You shall know that your tent is in peace" (Job 5:24).

—Babylonian Talmud, *Y'vamot* 62b

When I was a little girl growing up in Norfolk, Virginia, each Sunday morning I attended religious school at Ohef Sholom Temple, where my father was the rabbi. Aside from the sugar cookies served at snack time, the best part of religious school was "assembly." For the last few minutes of each session, all of the classes would go to the chapel and meet for a brief service, a song session, and everyone's favorite, "Ask the Rabbi." For those ten minutes of "Ask the Rabbi," my father became every child's dad.

Inviting the children to ask him anything they wished, my father opened himself up to questions such as "How much do you weigh, Rabbi Forman?" and "Is that your real hair?" Quickly, the questions would become more serious: "What makes a lobster unkosher?" "If we are Reform, are we really Jewish?" "Why is there war?" "Was there really a Moses like the Bible says?" "Why are we Jewish?" "Where is God?"

"I'm so glad you asked. . . ," my father would tell each student. Then he would try to answer. The chapel turned still and quiet. Perhaps the most important part of the two and a half hours of religious school each week was the ten minutes of "Ask the Rabbi."

Now I am an adult, a parent, and a rabbi. For seven years I served as the director of the religious school at Manhattan's Temple Shaaray Tefila. A great portion of my time was devoted to heart-to-heart talks with hundreds of young people about their Jewish questions as well as conversations with parents about raising Jewishly literate children. The parents in our school of seven-hundred students were well-educated, articulate, and seldom tongue-tied when asked difficult questions by their children. On subjects such as adoption, war, and sexuality, the parents served as able interpreters for their children as they broke down complex issues, filtered them through their own worldview, and then crystallized digestible, meaningful answers for their families. However, in spite of their sophistication, the parents were often anxious and reluctant to answer their children's most basic Jewish questions in a similar manner. Many of the phone calls I received from parents were not about Hebrew homework. Parents hungered to know how to answer their children's Jewish questions with intellectual and spiritual honesty in ways that were developmentally suitable. Often unsure of their own scattered Jewish knowledge, parents resorted quickly to a very traditional party line as they answered children's questions about God, prayer, Jewish holidays, and customs. When their children turned eight or nine, suddenly parents were surprised that their little ones felt duped and confused about Jewish ideas. God isn't a man in the sky? The Red Sea parting might have been a muddy Sea of Reeds? Not all Jewish people express being

Jewish the way their family does? These questions challenged the most erudite of parents. "What do I tell the kids?" they asked me.

A parent must fulfill so many different jobs in the course of the day: teacher, maid, chauffeur, nurse, coach. Jewish parents must also help their children grow into their Jewish identity by answering questions for which their own backgrounds may not have prepared them. This book has been written to assist parents in answering some of the questions that seem to puzzle so many of our children. *Honest Answers to Your Child's Jewish Questions: A Rabbi's Insights* serves as a bridge connecting facts, traditions, and history from the adult world to the world of a child. There are a multitude of excellent resources giving factual answers to basic questions of Jewish knowledge: "When do we celebrate the Jewish New Year?" "What is a latke?" Unlike the many wonderful books answering questions of "how" and "when," this book aims to answer questions of "why" and "why me." Walking parents and educators through the difficult terrain of children's theological and religious questions in accessible language, this book is a guide rather than an encyclopedia. It is not intended to serve as a comprehensive introduction to Judaism for parents or substitute for a well-rounded and joyful Jewish education for children. *Honest Answers* is one tool among many to help parents find the words to make Judaism meaningful for their children. Whether the reader is a parent, a religious school teacher, or even a member of the clergy, this book helps adults confront the powerful questions children ask from a liberal Jewish perspective.

Honest Answers categorizes over fifty frequently asked questions into seven chapters:

• Jewish Identity and Jewish Learning
• God

- The Jewish Life Cycle
- The Bible
- Israel
- Anti-Semitism
- Jewish Diversity

Certainly, each chapter could serve as subject matter for an entire book. Yet a short answer is often just what a child is looking for to satisfy his or her curiosity. Longer answers written for an early elementary school–aged child are provided for some of the more complicated topics. These answers supply additional information to parents or teachers, who may wish to edit out extraneous facts for younger children. At the start of each chapter, an essay encapsulating some of the major themes of the chapter is addressed to adult readers. Parents are encouraged to use their discretion and judgment when responding to such emotionally charged topics as death and God. Parents know their children better than anyone. Their sensitivity in presenting this and any information to their child's growing mind is crucial. A reader need not follow the book's order and may easily flip from chapter to chapter, if desired. A glossary provides easy reference for some of the Hebrew terms referred to in the book. A brief selection of suggested readings is included at the end of each chapter to help parents and children explore these topics further.

In the midst of the busy schedules that families maintain, the notion of why a child is bothering to learn to decipher the Hebrew language or why a family chooses to affiliate with a particular synagogue may become lost or unarticulated. It is my goal to remind children, parents, and educators that parents give us a Jewish identity and education out of a sense of love and a conviction that Judaism is immensely precious and worthy of carrying on through the generations. When parents believe that living a Jewish life involves choices rather than clearly defined God-given mandates, answering children's questions becomes that much more challenging. I hope to make this part of Jewish parenting just a bit easier.

Perhaps this book can help you and your family tap into a sense of joy in your own journey of Jewish discovery. Here is a guide to help you share some important answers with children you care about. I'm so glad you asked.

Acknowledgments

Several hands and hearts assisted in the birth of this book.

Thanks to Rabbi Hara Person, my editor at the URJ Press, for her gentle guidance and overall vision of this book. Without Hara's intelligence and encouragement, this manuscript would not exist. Hara was helped to bring this book to publication by the staff of the URJ Press, including Victor Ney, Michael Goldberg, Ron Ghatan, Lauren Dubin, Debra Hirsch Corman, and Zachary Kolstein. I would also like to thank Julie Vanek, RJE, of Temple Shalom, Newton, Massachusetts, and Rabbi Vered Harris, RJE, of Congregation Beth Torah, Overland Park, Kansas, for their generous help reviewing and commenting on an early draft of this book.

Thank you also to the staff at Temple Shaaray Tefila in New York City for their support and enthusiasm. A special debt of gratitude is owed to Sari Luck Schneider, Temple Shaaray Tefila's director of early childhood programs, who read and commented on an early draft of the book, and to Elizabeth R. Gross, who provided constant encouragement before a book was ever written. Rachelle Friedman, Reyna Marder Gentin, Kim Hoelting, Cantor

Jenny Izenstark, and Rabbi Valerie Leiber lent their insight and encouraging voices.

For his perceptive comments and for taking the time to read early drafts of chapters with painstaking attention, I cannot thank my big brother, Rabbi Joseph M. Forman, enough. His excellent skills as a writer and his expertise in areas of philosophy and Jewish history made him a perfect reader and editor. His corrections and suggestions spurred me to think about the issues discussed in the book more deeply and clearly. I am extremely grateful to him for his time and effort.

This book was written over vacations from work at Temple Shaaray Tefila and during my days off. I could never have taken the time away from my own children if they had not been in the gentle care of our beloved nanny, Somorne Harrison. Thank you for helping us in our endeavors to raise *menschen* and for being a wonderful teacher for our family.

I thank my family for their support and love of Judaism that have infused the writing of this book: my mother, Vivian Fish Forman; my father, Rabbi Lawrence A. Forman; my siblings and their families, Dr. Julie Forman-Kay, Dr. Lewis Kay, Raphael and Shira Kay, Rabbi Joseph Forman, and Cantor Alisa Forman. Anne Loeb Marx and Henry Marx, Dr. Jeffrey Marx and Heidi Epstein, Joelle and Jordan Marx, thank you as well, for your encouragement and for sharing your incredible stories.

Finally, I thank my husband, Dr. Steven Marx, for providing me with the love and moral support that enabled me to write this book. Constantly, I am inspired by his love of family and his commitment to the mysteries and questions of science. For our children, Abigail, Joshua, and Benjamin, may you find meaningful answers to all of your questions and enjoy all of the beautiful discoveries yet to be.

Honest
Answers

TO YOUR CHILD'S

Jewish
Questions

✦ ✦ ✦

Chapter 1

JEWISH IDENTITY
AND JEWISH LEARNING

- Why am I Jewish?
- What is important about being Jewish?
- Why do I have to go to religious school and receive a Jewish education?
- Why should I learn Hebrew?
- Why should I become a bar or bat mitzvah?
- What is a synagogue?
- Why do we go to synagogue?
- What does a rabbi do?
- What does a cantor do?
- If one of my parents is not Jewish, am I really Jewish?
- If I am adopted, am I really Jewish?
- Is there a Jewish way to behave?
- Why don't we celebrate Christmas?

This first chapter begins where so many of our children begin their questioning, from their own experiences. Why am I Jewish?

Why do I have to attend religious school? Why must I learn Hebrew? Why am I going to synagogue? All of us begin to learn by understanding who we are and how the world works in relationship to us. We begin life completely attached to our mothers' bodies. Growing up means separating physically and emotionally and recognizing that each of us is a unique individual. As we grow older and mature, we attempt to understand the world from perspectives outside of our own personal experiences. When we can once again see ourselves as attached or linked to our community and families, we have experienced additional growth.

At the Passover seder we read the tale of the four children—one wise, one wicked, one simple, and one unable to ask a question. The Passover Haggadah encourages us to answer our children according to their needs. The "wise" child hungers for facts and history, while the "simple" child can only look around him or her and wonder, "What is this?" The "wicked" child asks, "What does this service mean to you?" revealing his or her alienation from the Jewish community. And of course, some children do not even know how to articulate a question. As parents, we can prevent the isolation of the so-called "wicked" child by breaking our silence about Judaism. We can fill our children with a sense that Judaism is a precious part of who we are. Each time a question is asked, we can answer it more fully. First, we paint broad brushstrokes with our answers, creating a large picture. Then, as the questions are repeated, our answers become more finely tuned. We can expand the detail of our answers. We can fill in the gaps. We can create answers of beauty, depth, and meaning that help our children better understand their Jewish identities.

✦ ✦ ✦

Why am I Jewish?

You are Jewish because one or both of your parents is Jewish, and they have passed that religion on to you. From all of the religions in the world, your parents have chosen to make the Jewish religion part of your family's life. Being Jewish is a beautiful gift. Being Jewish makes you part of a group of people who are connected because they are Jewish too. Being Jewish reminds us to treasure the passing days, weeks, and months as we mark time with Jewish celebrations and customs.

Judaism is a religion that is passed down from great-great-great-great-great-grandparents (and even earlier) all the way to your parents and finally to you. People can also choose to become Jewish. Whether your parents were born Jewish or chose to become Jewish, one day you will be able to pass your Judaism down to your children. Imagine that Judaism is like a beautiful chain. Each generation adds a link to the chain and then gives the chain to their children for safekeeping. Your parents have given you this precious chain. When you learn about Judaism and live a Jewish life, you are adding your own special link. Even if you are one of the first people in your family to live a Jewish life, you will be part of a long, long chain of people who have been Jewish and have been proud of this tradition.

What is important about being Jewish?

No two people on earth are exactly the same. Even identical twins have differences. What is important to one person about being Jewish may not be the same as what is important to someone else. Being Jewish is important to different people for different reasons.

For hundreds and hundreds of years, Jewish people have felt the responsibility to make the world better. In a language called Hebrew, repairing the world is called *tikkun olam*. Although good people of many different religions help make the world a better place, Jewish people have special words and ways of fixing the world, or doing *tikkun olam*. Our Torah and other important books from many years ago suggest ways of doing things like visiting sick people, celebrating with people who are getting married, or giving comfort to people who are sad because someone they love is sick or has died. Being Jewish means that you are someone who can fix the world in a special way, with customs and ideas that have been around for many, many years and also new traditions to help fix some of the problems our world may have. For some people, *tikkun olam* is the most important part about being Jewish.

Other people might say that what is important about being Jewish is doing the mitzvot, the commandments in the Torah that God gave to the Jewish people. The rabbis who lived a long time ago taught that there are 613 mitzvot, or commandments, in the Torah. These commandments include rules about eating certain kinds of foods, not stealing, and not hurting other people. There are many other commandments as well as customs that a person may keep as a Jew. Different Jews have different opinions about whether or not and how to observe these mitzvot.

For some people, the most important thing about being Jewish is living a Jewish life. When you attend a Jewish preschool or religious school or day school, attend Shabbat services, use Jewish ritual objects in your home like a mezuzah on your door, celebrate Shabbat with your family, read a Jewish story, celebrate the Jewish holidays, or participate in acts of kindness and responsibility in your community (such as giving *tzedakah* or visiting people who are sick), you are

living a Jewish life. Living a Jewish life is meant to bring more meaning and purpose to your life.

All religions give people a way of thinking about the world and a
way of asking and answering questions about life. There are many
religions in the world. Religions teach us about how we are supposed
to treat each other and how we can understand what happens to us.
Religions also teach us ideas about God and how the world was born
or created. Different religions teach us to pray or talk to God and one
another in special ways. Religions also have certain ways or customs
to celebrate different times of our lives like welcoming a new baby or
becoming a teenager. Being Jewish is your way. Being Jewish can be
an important part of who you are. Your parents hope that being
Jewish will help you grow up into a person who learns to be kind,
loving, and giving. This means being someone who cares about all
people, no matter what their race or religion, and being the kind of
person who feels a special attachment to the community of Jewish
people.

Why do I have to go to religious school and receive a Jewish education?

Your parents want you to learn what Jewish people have been
thinking about and talking about for over four thousand years.
Parents have the job of giving their children something called a
"religious identity." This means that your parents want you to
know and understand your religion. When your parents send you
to religious school, they are giving you a Jewish education and
helping you grow up understanding yourself. The values or ideas
that you explore in religious school will make you a stronger person. Just as your parents give you vitamins and healthy foods to

help make your body strong and help you grow, they send you to school to help your mind grow. In religious school, you will learn about the Torah, the most important Jewish book, as well as other Jewish books and writings. You will also learn about Jewish prayers and what they teach us about life, and ways to act with kindness toward other people and the world around you. Religious school also helps you learn about being Jewish when you are not in your synagogue. You will learn about celebrating Jewish holidays and about the meaning of Jewish customs and traditions.

Our Bible (*Tanach* in Hebrew) has in it a book called Proverbs. The Book of Proverbs offers advice about acting wisely. Proverbs teaches that studying Torah (and Jewish learning in general) can help us in our lives: "When you walk, it will guide you; when you lie down, it will watch over you; and when you awake, it will speak to you" (Proverbs 6:22). Your parents cannot always be with you. When you learn about Judaism, your parents know that you will be able to make wise decisions in the challenges you face every day, even if they are not there to help you.

It is a Jewish value to study with others and learn from everyone. Your parents have chosen for you to learn in your religious school with other young people. Although sometimes it is good to spend time alone, Jewish people have believed for centuries that we need to spend some time together. In this way we can learn from each other and take care of each other. One of the great rabbis used to say: "Do not separate yourself from your community" (*Pirkei Avot* 4:5). When you go to religious school, you become part of the Jewish community.

Your parents may tell you unpleasant stories about their Jewish education when they were growing up. They may tell you that they resisted going to religious school or that they misbehaved in Hebrew class. Some parents even seem proud of these stories about what they had to put up with. Your religious school experience is probably very different from that of your parents. Today's religious schools are run by well-trained educators who understand that children have busy lives and long school days. Your teachers and religious school educators work hard to teach you in creative and interesting ways. Religious schools today are very different than when your parents were growing up!

Going to religious school is worthwhile for so many reasons. You will learn more about yourself, your family, your community, your history. You will be encouraged to take part in programs that improve the world. You will make Jewish friends with whom you can have fun and share being Jewish. Especially if you live in an area or go to a school where there aren't a lot of Jews, religious school is a place to be with other Jewish students and experience a connection based on your common heritage. You can celebrate being Jewish at the same time that you figure out your personal beliefs.

Why should I learn Hebrew?

Hebrew, or *Ivrit*, has always been the common language of Jews around the world. Learning Hebrew is a way to understand prayers and readings from the Bible firsthand without having to rely on someone else's translation. Yet Hebrew is not only a connection to our past. Hebrew is also the language of the modern State of Israel. We also learn Hebrew because it helps us connect with Jews in Israel and all around the world.

Hebrew has always been considered a sacred and important part of Jewish identity. Depending on what country a Jew lives in, he or she might have an English name, a French name, a Spanish name, or a Russian name. When Jewish babies are born, it is customary for parents to also give them a Hebrew name. For example, a Jewish boy in America might be called Jake, and a Jewish boy in Argentina might be called Jacobo, but in Hebrew both of them are called Yaakov. Having a Hebrew name connects you with the history of your family, with Jewish history, and with all Jews everywhere.

Knowing how to write and read your Hebrew name, being able to read a verse from the Torah in Hebrew, knowing how to read a prayer in Hebrew from any prayer book anywhere in the world are all part of the privilege of learning this ancient Jewish language. Learning Hebrew is an exciting part of being Jewish.

Most of the important Jewish books, such as the Torah, Prophets, Mishnah, and commentaries, are written in Hebrew. Hebrew was the language that Jews spoke in Israel thousands of years ago and have continued to use for prayer, study, and even business agreements no matter where in the world they lived. Even though Jews were spread out all across the world and spoke many different languages, Hebrew was the common Jewish language that Jews could use to communicate.

When Jews started to return to the Land of Israel in the late 1800s, it became important for there to be one common language. These pioneers were committed to using the ancient language of Hebrew for their new life in the Land of Israel. Eliezer Ben-Yehuda, who lived from 1858–1922, believed that Hebrew should become a modern language. He created a dictionary that helped to make the Hebrew language one that could be used not just for prayers or synagogue, but for everyday life. New words were invented for things that didn't exist in biblical times, like "airplane," "library," and "clock." Hebrew was transformed into a language that could be used all of the time, in the doctor's office, in school, in the playground, and in the newspaper, as well as at synagogue. Hebrew became a living language. Today, Jews continue to learn Hebrew because it is the language of our most precious literature and history.

Why should I become a bar or bat mitzvah?

We usually associate bar or bat mitzvah with lots of studying, reading from the Torah, and having a big party. But surprisingly, whether or not you celebrate this milestone at a synagogue, you officially become a bar or bat mitzvah simply by reaching the age of thirteen years and one day. This means that you will become a bar or bat mitzvah whether or not you study a Torah portion, lead services in a synagogue, or have a party.

Becoming a bar or bat mitzvah is a little like turning eighteen years old in the United States. As soon as your eighteenth birthday happens, you automatically have certain rights and responsibilities, such as being allowed to vote. *Bar mitzvah* means "one obligated to the mitzvot, or commandments." A Jewish person who has reached the status of bar or bat mitzvah has certain privileges in Jewish life, such as being counted in a minyan (prayer quorum), and has certain obligations, such as not eating on Yom Kippur. This official entrance into the world of adult Jewish responsibility has been taking place for hundreds of years.

Becoming a bar mitzvah was traditionally marked with an *aliyah*, the privilege of being called up to recite the blessing over the reading of a portion of the Torah in a religious service. That act showed that the young man was growing up and ready to take on more Jewish obligations. Until the early twentieth century, it was a ritual in which only boys participated. In 1921, Judith Kaplan became the first young woman in America to have this kind of public celebration of becoming a bat mitzvah, literally a "daughter of the commandment." She chanted the blessings over the Torah and read from the Bible at the Society for the Advancement of Judaism, the synagogue in New York City where her father was the rabbi. In many synagogues today, there is no difference between a bar or a bat mitzvah.

But why go through the process of study and preparation for becoming a bar or bat mitzvah if all you have to do is turn thirteen? Those who have celebrated becoming a bar or bat mitzvah in front of their congregation, family, and friends have said that it is one of the most exciting days of their lives. They have the chance to show that they are part of a long chain of Jewish tradition, going back many generations. One or both of their parents may have read from the Torah at their own ceremony years before. Grandfathers, great-grandfathers, and great-great-grandfathers celebrated bar mitzvah. When young people read from the Torah, they know that they are part of a tradition of learning and part of a bigger family of the Jewish people.

Studying and preparing to become a bar or bat mitzvah also gives you the chance to be Jewish in new ways. It means you are old enough to study the Torah in depth and really get to know this piece of our legacy. The Torah is divided into fifty-four different portions, and each portion is assigned to a particular Shabbat of the year. The portion of the Torah that you study will always belong to you in a special way. Every year, on the Shabbat when that portion is read, it will be "your portion."

The process of studying and preparing to become a bar or bat mitzvah allows you to learn new skills that will help you live a Jewish life. It is a time to think about what being Jewish means to you. It is also a time to think about how becoming a bar or bat mitzvah can inspire you to help others now and for the rest of your life.

At first it might seem overwhelming to stand in front of an entire congregation and read or chant parts of the service, the Torah, and haftarah. But your cantor, rabbi, or teacher will help make sure that you are properly prepared. When you lead services, you may feel like you are in a play or recital, but it is very different. You do not have to "perform perfectly," and you do not have to act. You just have to do your best and show what you have learned. In doing so, you are doing your part to help continue Judaism.

What is a synagogue?

The word "synagogue" comes from a Greek word meaning "assembly" or "gathering." It is a building where Jews gather to worship or pray. Three thousand years ago, Jews had a large temple in Jerusalem where they made sacrifices and worshiped God. This temple, called the Temple or the First Temple, was built by King Solomon. About twenty-five hundred years ago, in the year 586 B.C.E., the Temple in Jerusalem was destroyed by the Babylonians. A new temple, called the Second Temple, was later built where the First Temple had stood. During the time of the Second Temple, some of the people who had previously lived in the kingdom of Judea lived in other parts of the world. Although they may have sent taxes to the Temple in Jerusalem and come to visit the Temple on the Three Pilgrimage Festivals (Sukkot, Passover, and Shavuot), they built synagogues in their new hometowns. In these local synagogues, they were able to pray, spend time together, and study. Today, our temples or synagogues serve a similar role. They are houses of prayer, houses of study, and places for Jews to come together.

Why do we go to synagogue?

We go to synagogue for many different reasons. The synagogue, or temple, is where Jews go to pray. In the first book of the Torah, the Book of Genesis, God tells the first human being, "It is not good that the man should be alone" (Genesis 2:18). Jewish tradition teaches that even though a Jew can pray alone, a full prayer service requires a group of at least ten adults called a minyan. When Jews go to synagogue, we are not alone.

We also go to synagogue to learn and to study about Judaism. Many synagogues have classes for adults as well as children. People can learn about the Torah or other important Jewish books. They may take classes in Jewish cooking or Israeli dancing. Sometimes adults attend bar and bat mitzvah classes if they never had a chance to do so when they were younger. Children may go to synagogue for preschool, religious school, or Jewish high school. Some synagogues have Jewish day schools where children go every day to learn about Jewish subjects as well as other subjects like science and math and music. The synagogue is where we can learn more about who we are.

Jews also go to synagogue to celebrate special occasions like the naming of Jewish babies, consecration (the entrance of children into religious school and Jewish learning), an individual becoming a bar or bat mitzvah, or a Jewish wedding. Sometimes we go to synagogues for sad occasions like funerals or on *yahrzeits,* the anniversaries of the deaths of people we loved.

The temple or synagogue is also a place to be with our Jewish friends. Many synagogues have playgroups for toddlers or tot Shabbat programs. Synagogues also have youth groups, which are clubs in which young people can have fun together and do projects that help the community. They might go apple picking, ice-skating, or have a toy drive for children who wouldn't otherwise get gifts at holiday time. Adults also make friends in synagogue and often meet for classes, projects, and programs.

Many synagogues also help out their neighborhoods by being a place for different community groups to meet, such as support groups for people who are suffering from certain kinds of illnesses or for people who have had sad things happen to them. Some synagogues have homeless shelters, where people who do not have homes can live for a while or where they can sleep at night.

The synagogue is so much more than a building. A synagogue is a place where Jews can be part of a Jewish community and can reach out to the larger community in which they live.

What does a rabbi do?

The word *rabbi* means "teacher," and that is a rabbi's most important job. A rabbi helps Jewish people learn about Judaism. Many rabbis work in a synagogue and help lead worship services. At services, the rabbi may lead prayers, teach about the weekly Torah portion, or give a talk about an important idea. A rabbi helps welcome new Jewish babies into the community by saying special blessings and prayers and giving the baby a Hebrew name. When two people decide to get married, they speak with their rabbi, and the rabbi officiates (is in charge) at the wedding. Rabbis also visit people in the hospital or at home if they are sick or lonely. When someone is at the end of his or her life, the rabbi can help him or her say good-bye. The rabbi also helps to comfort that person's family and friends at a special service called a funeral. The rabbi is someone you can speak with if you have a problem.

Some rabbis work in places other than synagogues. They may write books or teach at a college. Other rabbis teach in Jewish schools or work in hospitals providing comfort to the patients and their families. Some rabbis work in office buildings where they publish Jewish books, or they are in charge of organizations that help Jewish people around the world. Some rabbis even run Jewish summer camps.

Rabbis spend a great deal of time studying about the ideas and history of the Jewish people. They study the Hebrew language. They study the important Jewish books and the ideas of great thinkers. Rabbis also learn how to help people who are scared, upset, worried, or sick or who may need some guidance. Learning how to give sermons and how to be a good teacher are also important parts of learning to be a rabbi. Rabbis do many different things each day. You can ask the rabbi at your temple about his or her job and what he or she likes best about it.

What does a cantor do?

The cantor is a person who, like a rabbi, helps Jewish people learn about Judaism. The Hebrew word for a male cantor is *chazan*, and the word for a female cantor is *chazzanit*. Our English word, "cantor," comes from the Latin language and means "to sing." Cantors study for many years to learn all of the special melodies or songs in the service. They learn all of the tunes for chanting or singing the different books of the Bible as well as the special music to help with naming babies, weddings, and other occasions in people's lives. Often, the cantor's main job is to help lead prayers and singing during Jewish services. In addition to singing, many cantors know how to play musical instruments.

Cantors can do other things as well. Many cantors spend a great deal of time teaching bar and bat mitzvah students. The cantor may be in charge of a choir at the synagogue too. Cantors help people feel at home in their synagogue. Like rabbis, cantors officiate at weddings, baby namings, and funerals, visit people in the hospital, and teach classes about Judaism.

If one of my parents is not Jewish, am I really Jewish?

In the Reform Movement, you are considered Jewish even if one of your parents is not Jewish. As long as you are receiving a Jewish education and participate in Jewish life-cycle events (such as having a baby naming, becoming a bar or bat mitzvah, or having a confirmation ceremony), you are Jewish.

According to traditional Jewish law (halachah), you are really Jewish only if your mother is Jewish. Conservative and Orthodox Jews believe that being Jewish is passed on from mothers to their children from one generation to the next. Therefore, if your father is Jewish and your mother is not Jewish, you would need to study about Judaism and participate in a ceremony called "conversion" in which you would officially declare your Jewish identity and say that you are now Jewish.

The Reform Movement has a different way of thinking about this important question. Since 1983, the Reform Movement has officially accepted an idea that says it does not matter which one of your parents is Jewish.

If I am adopted, am I really Jewish?

If you are adopted, you are considered to be your parents' child. Parents are parents, whether they are biological or adoptive. The

Talmud teaches that "whoever brings up an orphan in his home, Scripture views it as though he was his own child" (Babylonian Talmud, *Sanhedrin* 19b). But just as children who were born outside of the United States or Canada have to officially become citizens of the country of their adoptive parents, so too do children born of non-Jewish birth parents usually do something that "officially" makes them Jewish.

Some rabbis do not require that children who are adopted by Jewish parents go through a special ceremony or ritual of conversion. These rabbis believe that when parents give their children a Jewish education, Jewish values, and celebrate Jewish life-cycle events and traditions with them, this is all the parents need to do in order to give them a Jewish identity. Other rabbis do require that children who are adopted go through a formal conversion ceremony. This way their Jewish identity can never be questioned later on in their lives.

When a child goes through a conversion ceremony, he or she is taken to a *mikveh*, a ritual bath. One of the parents goes in the warm water with the child and dips him or her three times in the water. A blessing is recited in front of three rabbis or knowledgeable Jewish people. The child is then given a Hebrew name. When the child becomes old enough to become a bar or bat mitzvah, he or she makes a public decision about being Jewish. By chanting the blessing before and after the reading of the Torah, the young person shows that he or she truly wishes to be Jewish.

Is there a Jewish way to behave?

We behave Jewishly when we act in ways that reflect the teachings of the Torah, the writings and rules of the rabbis, and the wisdom of our sages, both of long ago and today. What that means exactly though is more complicated. Jews come from every corner of the world, and we all have different customs and traditions. There have also been different ideas throughout Jewish history about how to behave. Because there are so many different Jews and Jewish ideas, it is impossible to describe only one right way of behaving Jewishly. For some Jews, behaving Jewishly means following as many of the Jewish laws (called halachah*)* as possible. Some of these laws talk about how to treat people, like showing respect for older people or not tripping blind people. Other laws teach rules for praying and even eating. For other Jews, behaving Jewishly means following those rules that are meaningful and relevant. But there are some values that have been important to all Jews for hundreds and hundreds of years. Jews have tried to live by these values for many generations.

These Jewish behaviors can be summed up in three categories:

1. Torah—studying Jewish texts
2. *Avodah*—praying in a Jewish way
3. *G'milut chasadim*—living an ethical life

The actions that result from these three basic behaviors include helping others; acting with justice and mercy; showing honor and respect to parents, teachers, and those who are older; giving *tzedakah*; loving peace and trying to make peace in the world; studying and learning about Jewish history, culture, Hebrew language, Jewish books, and ideas; having a Jewish home; being part of a synagogue community; celebrating the Jewish holy days; and marking the moments of one's life in a Jewish fashion.

Mostly, behaving Jewishly means acting like a mensch. *Mensch* is the Yiddish word for "human being." Acting like a mensch means that you are acting the way a human being should act. In many ways, human beings are animals just like dogs or cats or monkeys. But in other ways, human beings are special and different from animals. We are capable of understanding the difference between what is good and bad, right and wrong. A mensch works hard to make decent and kind choices. None of us is perfect, and we don't always act the best way we can. But as Jews we have to try our best to act like *menschen* (Yiddish for "mensches"). When we act like mensches, we don't do something just because it feels good at that moment. We try to do the right and kind thing. Almost two thousand years ago, our teacher and rabbi, Hillel, taught, "In a place where there are no human beings, struggle to be a human being" (*Pirkei Avot* 2:5). When people are acting cruelly or thoughtlessly, it is our job to behave in the finest way that a human being can act. Being a mensch is an important part of behaving in a Jewish way.

Why don't we celebrate Christmas?

Christmas is a wonderful, joyous holiday celebrated by Christians around the world. This holiday marks the birthday of Jesus, a teacher who lived in the northern part of Israel over two thousand years ago. Jews and Christians share important values such as praying for peace. But sharing certain beliefs does not mean we are the same. Jews and Christians do not believe in the same religious ideas. Christians believe that Jesus was very special. They believe that he was the son of God and that he was much more than a regular person. For Christians, Jesus is the Christ or "savior."

Jesus taught people that God would be in charge of life on earth soon and would get rid of difficult times. The Romans who were in charge of the Land of Israel at that time believed that Jesus and his ideas were dangerous. They killed Jesus in a very cruel way, called crucifixion. Some people believed that after three days, his body was miraculously given new life and he rose up to heaven to God. About one hundred years later, a religion called Christianity came into being. Christianity is based on Jesus and his teachings and teaches that Jesus will come back to earth some day.

No matter how important a teacher Jesus was, Jews do not believe that he was God's special son. Jewish people believe that every human being is God's special child. Jews also don't believe that Jesus was our savior who will someday bring about a time of heaven on earth. We believe that human beings must work together to bring about a time when there will be peace and goodness and righteousness on earth. For all these reasons, it is not Jewish to celebrate Jesus's birthday.

It can be a lot of fun to join with friends and family in their celebration of Christmas. We can help to hang beautiful ornaments on their Christmas tree, exchange gifts, and enjoy lovely music. You might have some relatives who are Christian and celebrate Christmas. There's nothing wrong with sharing in someone else's Christmas celebration. Just as we go to our friends' birthday parties and give them gifts on their special day, we can give gifts to our Christian friends or relatives on Christmas and help them celebrate their special time of the year. But just as a friend's birthday is not our birthday, Christmas is not a Jewish holiday

There are parts of celebrating Christmas that we might even like to bring into our home. Yet Christmas is a special day for Christians. If we borrow some of its customs, it is like we are telling our Christian friends that we can use these customs without believing the meaning behind them. This does not show the highest respect for Christianity or for Judaism.

Resources for Further Reading on Jewish Identity and Jewish Learning

BOOKS FOR ADULTS

The First Jewish Catalog: A Do-It-Yourself Kit, edited by Michael Strassfeld. Jewish Publication Society, 1989.

The How to Handbook for Jewish Living, by Kerry Olitzky and Ronald Isaacs. KTAV Publishing House, 1993.

If I'm Jewish and You're Christian, What Are the Kids? A Parenting Guide for Interfaith Families, by Andrea King. UAHC Press, 1993.

The Jewish Book of Why, by Alfred J. Kolatch. Jonathan David Publishers, 2000.

Jewish Family & Life: Traditions, Holidays, and Values for Today's Parents and Children, by Yosef I. Abramowitz and Susan Silverman. Golden Books, 1997.

The Jewish Family Fun Book: Holiday Projects, Everyday Activities, and Travel Ideas with Jewish Themes, by Danielle Dardashti and Roni Sarig. Jewish Lights Publishing, 2002.

The Jewish Holidays: A Guide and Commentary, by Michael Strassfeld. HarperCollins, 1985.

The Jewish Home, by Daniel Syme. URJ Press, 2004.

Jewish Living: A Guide to Reform Practice, by Mark Washofsky. UAHC Press, 2000.

Putting God on the Guest List: How to Reclaim the Spiritual Meaning of Your Child's Bar or Bat Mitzvah, by Jeffrey K. Salkin. Jewish Lights Publishing, 1993.

The Second Jewish Book of Why, by Alfred J. Kolatch. Jonathan David Publishers, 1995.

Voices of Wisdom: Jewish Ideals and Ethics for Everyday Living, by Francine Klagsbrun. Jonathan David Publishers, 2001.

BOOKS FOR CHILDREN

A Child's First Book of Jewish Holidays, by Alfred J. Kolatch. Jonathan David Publishers, 1997.

The Jewish Child's First Book of Why, by Alfred J. Kolatch. Jonathan David Publishers, 1992.

The Jewish Kids Catalog, by Chaya Burstein. Jewish Publication Society, 1983.

For Kids—Putting God on Your Guest List: How to Reclaim the Spiritual Meaning of Your Bar or Bat Mitzvah, by Jeffrey K. Salkin. Jewish Lights Publishing, 1998.

What You Will See Inside a Synagogue, by Lawrence A. Hoffman and Ron Wolfson. Skylight Paths Publishing, 2004.

Chapter 2

GOD

- Do I have to believe in God to be Jewish?
- Who made God?
- Does God know everything?
- What does God look like?
- Is God a boy or a girl?
- Does God listen when I pray?
- Why should I pray if I don't think that God is listening?
- Why does God let terrible things happen?
- Is God Jewish?
- Does God like the Jewish people more than other people?

When my three-year-old daughter began to ask questions about God, I knew that a new milestone had been reached in her development and in our relationship. As parents, we are used to answering many questions with a sense of confidence. While it was easy for me to tell my daughter who my mommy and daddy were, it was not so easy to explain that in my understanding of God, there was no mommy or daddy for the Creator of the universe.

Speaking to our children about God can leave us tongue-tied. We are forced to confront our own beliefs about the universe, our own theologies, and our own doubts. For parents who were not raised as Jews yet are raising Jewish children, these kinds of questions may bring out lurking insecurity that we will give our children "wrong" answers and start them on their religious journeys with confusion rather than confidence.

Before attempting to divert your child's attention to another subject, or before you start reciting a juvenile theology that you abandoned years ago, take some time to think about your own questions and assumptions. What you believe matters. Clarifying your own God concept is an important step in being able to answer your child's questions. Perhaps now is a time to sit down with someone you respect and actually talk about God. What do you believe? What ideas will you not accept? Is God the force that created the universe? Does God play an active role in human history? Does God command us to study and live by the Torah, as discussed by the Rabbis who compiled the Mishnah and Talmud? Or do you believe that we live in dialogue with an ever-changing and growing God? Do you think that God is eternal? What are your doubts about God? Does God have a special relationship with the Jewish people? Why is there evil in the universe if God is good? Is God even necessarily good? Are there prayers in the prayer book that express your ideas perfectly? Are there prayers that speak of a God you cannot believe in?

In the Mishnah we read Rabbi Tarfon's words: "You are not required to complete the work, but neither are you free to desist from it" (*Pirkei Avot* 2:16). When our children begin the litany of "whys" and "hows" about God, we worry that we need to answer everything with the wisdom of a philosopher. But Rabbi Tarfon relieves us of that fear. You don't have to hold a doctorate in theology to begin to struggle with questions about God. It is a Jewish value to begin the hard work of figuring out what you believe and to examine your life and your actions closely. When you take time to talk to your child about what you believe, about your own questions, you are creating a powerful bond with your child. Your child can recognize that people have different ideas about God. You can help your child learn that ideas about God and life can and often do change as people mature; that sometimes people believe one thing when they are younger and something else when they get older. Teaching your child that it's not necessary to have all the answers, only to ask the questions, is an important lesson. The process of talking about God and other difficult concepts will set the tone for open communication with your child and let your child know that the two of you can talk about anything—even concepts that are hard for you to articulate.

This chapter includes ten frequently asked questions and answers regarding God. Though many books have been written on this topic, here the answers are brief in the hope that they will be enough to help you get a conversation started. These answers reflect an outlook that is respectful of tradition, yet grounded in the assertion that Judaism speaks with many voices. This multiplicity is part of the richness of Judaism. Moses Maimonides' concept of God is not the same as the God that Martin Buber understood. The Rabbis mentioned in the Mishnah and the Talmud have a different concept of God's listening to our prayers than does a modern thinker such as Abraham Joshua Heschel. The universal God of peace mentioned in the *Aleinu* prayer is a different kind of God from the God of Israel who rises over lesser gods in our *Mi Chamochah* prayer.

Traditional philosophies assume that God is omniscient (knows all), omnipotent (all-powerful), omnipresent (all-pervading), and omnibenevolent (all-kind). This concept of God may perplex us and our children when we face the wrongs and tragedies of life. Recognizing that human beings have created a multitude of ideas about God and that our notions of God are limited by our own human capacity for understanding may help us accept that we are still developing our own personal theologies. If we do not believe in the God of the Rabbis of the Mishnah, we can still be Jewish. In fact, Judaism is a religion whose God idea has changed throughout our thirty-five-hundred-year history. Our struggle to understand God is a noble one and is part of being a Jew.

A day came when we reached adulthood and our bodies stopped growing. Our minds, however, never stop growing. Our children and their questions ensure that this ongoing development never ceases.

✦ ✦ ✦

Do I have to believe in God to be Jewish?

Judaism has been around for over thirty-five hundred years. During this time, people have come up with unique ideas about God based on their experiences at different moments in history. You do not have to believe in one specific Jewish version of God to be Jewish. There are different Jewish ideas about God. When you were young, you might have believed in the kind of God who lives in the sky, or maybe you believed in a God who sits on a throne and watches all of your actions and writes down what you do in a big book. Perhaps you believed in the kind of God who sometimes answers your prayers "yes," and sometimes answers your prayers "no." Just as our ideas about God change as we grow, Judaism's ideas about God have changed as well.

Many of the ways that God is described in books or in pictures teach us about what God might be like rather than what God really is. Some of these ideas teach us what our ancestors thought about God. You might find, for example, that God is discussed as if God is a man. This doesn't mean that people actually thought that God was a man. But in the days when people in charge were always men, our ancestors couldn't imagine talking about something as powerful as God without using images or words connected to men. Today many people believe that when we talk about God as a man, this makes women feel left out or less important. The way we believe in God affects the way we treat ourselves and other people.

As a Jew, you are expected to do good deeds and follow some of the commandments whether or not you believe in God. Judaism teaches that actions are more important than belief. Doing good deeds is more important than believing whether a certain idea about God is true for you. It is more important to help make the world a better place than to believe in a specific kind of God.

Believing that God exists is a complicated idea. Being Jewish means you are asked to try to figure out what you believe and what makes sense for you. For many, many years, Jews have believed that there are no tree gods or rock gods or sun gods. For Jews, there is one central force that created the world, called God. But figuring out how God works in the world is not so easy for people to understand, and not every Jewish person agrees about God. By making the effort to study and learn and ask questions, you are doing the hard work of struggling to find your own personal belief. This struggle is important because it helps you grow and learn to appreciate the world in new ways. Wondering and doubting are not wrong. That is part of what makes you a thoughtful person. These are actually very Jewish things to do. Throughout history Jews have valued the process of thinking about God and the world.

All of our beliefs and ideas about God can change as we develop and grow. Do you remember what you thought about the world when you were three or four years old? How did you think that the sun moved in the sky? Did you understand why the moon changed its phase during the course of the month? Maybe you thought that waves in the ocean were caused by the movement of dolphins swimming through the water, or that there were little people living inside your television. As you grew older, you began to understand more about science and people and the natural laws of the world. Judaism gives us room to grow and change in our ideas about God. Part of being Jewish is trying to understand who and what God is. We're not expected to have all the answers to these questions. But we are expected to think about the questions and learn what other Jews have thought.

Who made God?

If you look around, you'll notice that everything came from somewhere. Trees come from seeds. Toys come from a store or factories. Cheese comes from milk. So where did God come from? There are many answers to this difficult question. You will have to decide which answer makes sense to you. Some people think that what makes God special is that God is the one and only thing in the entire universe that did not come from anything else. No one made God. God was here before anything else. God was always here. But that is only one answer. Some people believe that God was made up by the people who tried to understand the world. Because it was too hard to understand the world, people invented the idea of God to explain life.

According to rabbis who lived nearly two thousand years ago, God was not made by anyone. God has no parents. God is not a person. Some of these beliefs about God are expressed in Jewish prayers and songs. For the past six hundred years, Jewish people have been singing a song called *Adon Olam* when they pray in synagogue. In English, a*don* means "master," and *olam* means "forever." This prayer combines different ideas about God. It talks about God being "eternal," something that has been around forever. God has simply always been. God's power was around before the earth was created. God will always be.

Other prayers, like the *G'vurot*, express the idea that God is mighty like a hero. God can do anything. This prayer teaches that God can pick you up when you have fallen, heal you, free you, and keep you alive. In this prayer, God is the power that makes people alive.

There are also prayers like the *Mi Chamochah*. This prayer comes from the Torah, in the Book of Exodus. This prayer asks a question: "Who is like You, O God, among the gods that are worshipped?" This prayer says that our God is the best God of all of the other gods in the world. This prayer thinks about God differently from the other prayers in the prayer book that teach us that there is only one God.

The God in other parts of the Torah, like the Book of Deuteronomy, is a God who is similar to our parents. This is a God who blesses us when we make good choices and punishes us when we do something wrong. This section of the Torah teaches us that God goes before us, God will be with us, and God will not fail us or leave us alone. We are told not to be afraid or confused. We are told that if we obey God's voice, our lives will be fair and good. This biblical idea of God can bring us great comfort and assurance.

Who made God? Judaism teaches us that God was not made at a certain time. God has been around and goes on forever and ever. We say that God is "eternal." In some ways, people make up ideas about God and about what God wants from people. We can learn from these many ideas and, through them, discover our own thoughts about God.

Does God know everything?

What does God know? Does God know every answer to the questions on a math or science test? Can God see the future? If God knows everything, why does God ask Adam and Eve where they are in the Garden of Eden? If God knows everything that will happen, do people have any control over themselves? Are we free to make choices, or do we live inside some sort of movie, where God knows the ending, and we can't really decide how we are going to act?

Our ideas about God come from different places. Jewish and non-Jewish thinkers have written many books that deal with these exact questions. People have always wanted to know the answers. The Bible tells us some things about God's nature, God's names, and how to behave toward God. People like Philo Judaeus (20 B.C.E.–50 C.E.) wrote that God knows everything because God is the Mind of the universe or the Soul of the universe. These thinkers said that God is "omniscient." That means that God knows everything.

Philosophers like Moses Maimonides, who lived 1135–1204 and was also a doctor and rabbi, taught that we cannot truly understand God because our minds are not designed to comprehend all of what God is. Maimonides and other thinkers said that human beings have free will, which means that we can decide whether or not we are going to make good choices. People have self-control and imagination. Unlike other animals, we have the power to imagine the consequences of making one choice over another. We don't know whether or not God "knows everything." But most Jewish thinkers believe that we have the power to change parts of our lives.

What does God look like?

Since God is not a person, God does not have a body. We cannot know what God looks like. We cannot look at God with our eyes. But we can use our eyes to see God's creations.

Throughout time, people have tried to know what God is and what God looks like. In the Torah, in the third chapter of the Book of Exodus, God appears to Moses while he is taking care of his flocks of sheep. In this story, God calls to Moses from a bush that miraculously burns but is not burned up. The story tells us that when Moses turns to see this amazing sight, God calls to Moses from out of the bush. God says, "Moses, Moses." And Moses says, "Here I am." Moses hides his face, because he is afraid to look at God.

Like Moses, we do not see God's face. But we can see the power of God by looking at the miracles around us. Moses is able to understand more about God because he is able to notice what is amazing in the world around him. We cannot know what God looks like, but we can understand God better by using all of our senses to see what

God does. We can feel the wind, we can taste the fruit that grows on trees, we can see a rainbow, we can hear the sound of the ocean, we can smell flowers. We can know what God does by observing the world around us and by asking questions.

Blessings exist to help us appreciate wonders in our world. In our prayer service, we say "How great are Your works, O Eternal One! In wisdom You have formed them all, filling the earth with Your creatures." The philosopher Baruch Spinoza (1632–1677) wrote that God and the universe are one and the same. We can begin to "see" or understand God when we look at the wonders and the daily miracles in the universe.

Is God a boy or a girl?

God is not a person or a being with a face. God does not have a body and therefore does not have female or male body parts. God is not a boy or a girl. Moses Maimonides made a list of thirteen ideas about the Jewish faith in his commentary on the Mishnah. One of these ideas was that God does not have a form. Sometimes, we think of God as a man because when we discuss God, we often use words that describe God as "He" such as King, Father, Ruler, Master, or Lord.

Because we are people, we use words to describe ideas. The Bible is written in Hebrew. Hebrew is a language that does not have the word "it." Words that describe things or ideas in Hebrew have to be either male or female. Therefore, when we describe God using the Hebrew language, God's name has to be either male or female. Traditionally, Jews wrote and spoke about God as a male presence. For many Jews, the most powerful people in their lives were men: their fathers, their kings, their tribal leaders, and their teachers. We use ideas that are familiar to us to describe things that are difficult to understand. What we mean when we use those words is that God is *like* a king. God is *like* a father. God is *like* a ruler. God is *like* a person in charge. God is not actually any of these things. God is *like* these things.

There are prayers that describe God in other ways too—prayers that speak of mothers cradling us, or fathers protecting us. God can help us feel taken care of and safe, like a mother or father. But God is not really a mother or a father. God is not a person. God is not a boy or a girl.

Does God listen when I pray?

God does not have ears. Therefore God does not hear sounds the way that humans and other animals do. Yet we pray to God out loud. And some of the prayers speak about hoping that God hears us, just like we hope that our mother or father hears us when we ask for something.

Some Jewish people believe that God is like a mother or father who really does hear our words. They believe that our prayers travel up to heaven in the sky, and we are heard. Some of the prayers in the prayer book reflect this belief.

Many Jews believe that prayers are like poems. In this way of thinking, praying is different from asking for things from a parent. Prayer involves looking deeply inside of ourselves and thinking about what is important to us and our families and our community.

Prayer is a way to express thanks for the gifts in our lives. Prayers can give us comfort and reassure us that we will be okay. There is a prayer called the *Hashkiveinu* that does exactly this. This prayer tells us not to worry, that all will be well while we are sleeping, and we can look forward to waking up and being ready for a new day.

Prayer can also give us a chance to listen to ourselves and even have a conversation with ourselves. An important part of the Jewish worship service is the part devoted to silent prayer or meditation. At this moment, we hear our own voices. In the Bible (I Kings 19), we are taught that the prophet Elijah looked for God, but did not find God in earthquakes or wind or fire. Rather, Elijah found God in the still, small human voice. When we pray, we give that quiet voice within us the chance to be heard.

Many of our prayers are in Hebrew. Words like "I" and "me" do not usually appear in Jewish prayers. Jewish prayers talk about "us," "we," and "our." The words are not about one person, but rather about a group of people. We do not know if God "hears" us the way that human beings hear one another or hear music. But one thing that we know is that when Jews pray together, we can listen and learn to hear one another. The words of our prayers can inspire us to do better, behave well, and help other people.

When we pray, we don't know whether or not God hears us in a way we understand. But we can hear ourselves and each other, and we are able to change ourselves to be the best we can be. Our prayers can change us. Prayers can inspire us to do the work that will help others. We don't know how our prayers affect God. But we do know that praying can help us.

Why should I pray if I don't think that God is listening?

We cannot know if prayer has an effect on God. But we do know that praying can have a powerful effect on us. We are taught that our prayers are answered when they help us be better people. Even if we don't know that God is listening, we pray for some of these reasons:

1. The Hebrew word for prayer, *t'filah*, comes from a root that means "to judge oneself." Prayer can help you "judge yourself" and think about what you do and say so that you can be a better person. When you pray, you are reminded of your responsibility to help make the world a better place. Prayer helps you figure out what you can do to improve or even help God fix the world.

2. Prayer can help you figure out what is on your mind. Praying can help you take a few quiet moments out of your busy day to appreciate your life and blessings. Prayer is a way to say, "Thanks."

3. Prayer with other people helps you become part of a group of people who care about each other and look out for one another. Prayer reminds us that we're not alone.

4. Because Jews all over the world share the same prayers, prayer allows you to connect with the thoughts and wishes of Jews around the world. Prayer allows you to think about the lives of Jews throughout history who composed the prayers in our prayer book. Prayer helps you feel like you are part of the chain of Jewish tradition.

5. In prayers, God is described as compassionate, loving, truthful, protective, and listening. The Torah teaches us that people are created in God's image. When you pray, you remind yourself that you can choose to behave with those same qualities. Prayer reminds you to be the best person that you can be.

Why does God let terrible things happen?

If God is so great and strong and powerful, how could God let good people get sick or allow sad things to happen? This is a complicated question that Jews have asked for thousands of years. Some theologians, or thinkers about God, believe that God lets terrible things happen because God created nature in a certain way. Though God created nature, God doesn't control nature. The earth was created, and its surface grows and changes through earthquakes and volcanoes. Sometimes, people are hurt or killed by these forces of nature. People get sick because our bodies are made of matter that breaks down. God does not interfere in our lives, so when things fall apart for us, we must help each other. We cannot count on God to step in and change things.

Other theologians explain that terrible things happen because human beings have "free will" and have been created with the ability to make their own decisions. Sometimes people make bad decisions, and they hurt themselves or other people—for example, if they drive a car after drinking alcohol. Sometimes people make decisions that help make lives better, like being brave and telling someone the truth, or helping a friend who is hurt or sick. Either way, part of what makes us human is that we have the ability to make our own decisions. God doesn't control every move we make or how we choose to live our lives, even if that means that other people are hurt because of our decisions.

Still other theologians explain that God's ways are mysterious to people. Human beings cannot possibly understand God. We can wonder why bad things happen in the world, but we can never understand the reason. Rather, it is our job to respond to others and help them when tragedies occur and to prevent further tragedies. For example, when a flood occurs, we must respond by offering shelter, food, and medicine to those people who are suffering.

There is a book in the Bible called Job. Job was a good man, but he suffered terrible losses. He also experienced some miraculous happy events. Job asks God about the strangeness of life. There are no real answers given. Job says, "I spoke without understanding, of things beyond me, which I did not know" (Job 42:3). Life is so big and so perplexing that we cannot possibly understand everything.

What we do know is that we need to continue to use our minds to solve the mysteries of science so that we may help people who are sick. We know that we must use our minds and hearts to help bring about peace in the world so that people will not be hurt in wars. We need to use our minds and our resources to help make our world as safe as it can be so that tragedies can be prevented.

Despite all we know, we still have many questions about our world. Perhaps God is just not capable of helping us the way we might imagine a parent helping a child. Perhaps God's plan is not to get involved in the daily lives of human beings. Perhaps God watches us and wishes to help us. Some people believe God carries us through our difficult times. Other people believe that everything is God, both the good and the bad. There is no one right answer to these questions.

What we do know is that sometimes terrible things happen. We can learn to do our best to help take care of people who have suffered. We can also learn from our Bible to "teach us to number our days that we may get a heart of wisdom" (Psalm 90:12). We can think of every day as a very precious gift and appreciate our lives each moment.

Is God Jewish?

In the same way God does not have brown, curly hair or a Southern accent because God is not a person, God is not Jewish. God does not have any particular religion. If you are Jewish, you might think that God is Jewish too. But being Jewish means acting in the world in a certain way. God does not say prayers or read from the Torah or celebrate the Jewish festivals. Jewish people may worship God, but that does not make God Jewish. As Maimonides teaches, we cannot say that God has certain attributes. All we can say is that God is.

Does God like the Jewish people more than other people?

Throughout Jewish history, Jews have been referred to as "the chosen people." It is not easy to explain exactly what this means. God does not prefer the Jews to other people the way you might prefer pizza over string beans. In some Jewish stories and teachings, God is said to experience feelings. Because we can't understand God's actions, we use human terms to describe God or what God does. Even so, Jews do not believe that God experiences feelings or emotions the same way that human beings do.

In the Bible, the Jewish people are said to be special to God. Our tradition talks about the idea of the Jewish people being "chosen" by God to receive the Torah at Mount Sinai. Before and after the Torah is read in synagogue, a special blessing is chanted. This blessing praises God "who has chosen us from among the peoples, giving us this Teaching." This prayer explains that God gave the Torah to the Jewish people out of great love. On Friday evening, when we raise up *Kiddush* cups filled with grape juice or wine, the prayer that we recite talks about the holy Sabbath and about God's choosing of the Jewish people from all of the peoples of the world.

Other religious groups have not always liked the idea that the Jews were "chosen" by God to receive the Torah. But saying how good or special you are is a normal part of being human. When you write a card to your mother or father, you may say that they are "the best mom" or "the best dad" in the world. When you cheer for your school's basketball team, you may chant, "We are the best!" It is natural for people to want to feel good about themselves and their relationships with those around them.

Some of the prophets in the Bible explain that being chosen is actually a responsibility, not a special treat. Because we are chosen, Jewish people are required to be "a light to the nations." This means that Jewish people are supposed to help light up the world and guide everyone else to behave in a way that is just. The prophet Isaiah says that God has made Israel (another name for the Jewish people) God's servant. Israel has a job to do. This job is to be righteous and good. It is a special gift to be this "light," but it also requires hard work to make the world a better place and to help finish the work of Creation.

Some Jews do not agree with the term "the chosen people." They believe that when Jews call themselves "chosen" they are not being precise in describing their relationship with the Torah or with God. Some rabbis say that instead of being "the chosen people," Jews are really "the choosing people." Today, we choose to be Jewish and to live Jewish lives. Today, we choose to be a light to our families and our friends. We choose to live honorably. We choose to learn about being Jewish.

Resources for Further Reading on God

BOOKS FOR ADULTS

Finding God: Selected Responses, rev. ed., by Rifat Sonsino and Daniel B. Syme. UAHC Press, 2002.

A History of God: The 4,000-Year Quest of Judaism, Christianity, and Islam, by Karen Armstrong. Ballantine Books, 1994.

The Many Faces of God: A Reader of Modern Jewish Theologies, by Rifat Sonsino. URJ Press, 2004.

Teaching Your Children About God: A Modern Jewish Approach, by David J. Wolpe. Harper Perennial, 1995.

When Children Ask about God: A Guide for Parents Who Don't Always Have All the Answers, by Harold S. Kushner. Schocken Books, 1989.

BOOKS FOR CHILDREN

Because Nothing Looks Like God, by Lawrence Kushner and Karen Kushner. Jewish Lights Publishing, 2000.

God in Between, by Sandy Eisenberg Sasso. Jewish Lights Publishing, 1998.

God's Paintbrush, by Sandy Eisenberg Sasso. Jewish Lights Publishing, 1992.

Hello, Hello, Are You There God?, by Molly Cone, illustrated by Rosalind Charney Kaye. UAHC Press, 1999.

Chapter 3

THE JEWISH LIFE CYCLE

- What is a circumcision or bris?
- What is a baby naming?
- What is consecration?
- What is a bar or bat mitzvah?
- What is confirmation?
- What is conversion?
- What is a Jewish wedding?
- What happens when someone Jewish dies?
- What happens after we die?

Judaism is a response to life. The way we celebrate and honor the milestones of our lives defines us as human beings and as a community. In this chapter, you will find answers to some of the basic questions children ask regarding the Jewish life cycle. These answers are as direct and concise as possible.

The best way to truly teach your children about the Jewish life cycle is to include them in Jewish life-cycle experiences. Don't be reluctant to sit with your young child during a Shabbat service in which a bar or bat mitzvah is called to the Torah. These services are not meant to be private, but rather joyful communal prayer experiences in which a young person's newly achieved status is recognized. Having a mature child accompany you on a shivah visit, to help comfort mourners at home after a death, may be a powerful way to teach your child firsthand about the human capacity for compassion and kindness. Your children may surprise you with candid questions about death or the differences between a funeral and a memorial service. Answering the questions of a curious four year old about breaking a glass at a Jewish wedding may not require the same delicacy as explaining the concept of circumcision or the way that Jews deal with the rituals surrounding death. But whatever the question, your calm and honest responses will reassure your children and show them that Judaism can help guide us through life's passages.

Children learn best from experiencing rather than telling. No matter how mesmerizing or brilliant your child's school teachers may be, parents are the most powerful teachers and role models for their children. The Jewish life cycle provides an outlet for the many complicated and beautiful emotions that we feel as we make our journey through time.

✦ ✦ ✦

What is a circumcision or bris?

AN ANSWER FOR CHILDREN UNDER FIVE YEARS OLD

When a Jewish child is born, parents announce the name that they have picked for their child in front of friends and family. Jewish children also have a Hebrew name that parents choose for them. Some Jews use their Hebrew name all the time, while some use a different name for everyday use. In addition to getting a Hebrew name, when a Jewish boy is eight days old, he has what is called a circumcision. This is called a *bris* in Yiddish, or *b'rit milah* in Hebrew. At a bris, prayers are said to welcome the baby, the baby is given his Hebrew name, and the parents explain why they picked his name. At the bris, a person called a *mohel* or *mohelet* removes a small piece of skin on the baby's penis that doesn't have to be there. This procedure helps make him look like other Jewish boys and may help keep him more healthy. Many people who aren't Jewish don't remove this piece of skin, but in our Torah we read that God told Abraham that when a Jewish baby boy is born, this piece of skin should be removed when he is eight days old. It only takes a few moments for the *mohel* or *mohelet* to take away the piece of skin, and then everyone sings and welcomes the baby, says *mazal tov* (congratulations and good luck) to the baby's family, and has a little celebration.

AN ANSWER FOR CHILDREN OVER FIVE YEARS OLD

Circumcision is a procedure in which a piece of skin called the foreskin is cut away from the tip of a boy or man's penis. Many baby boys around the world have this procedure done to them in order to keep their penises cleaner or because of their family tradition. Many people who aren't Jewish don't remove this piece of skin, but we read in our Torah that God told Abraham that when a Jewish baby boy is born, this piece of skin should be removed when he is eight days old. Since that time, Jews have followed this mitzvah. Jewish boys are circumcised on the eighth day of their lives in a ceremony called a covenant of circumcision, *bris* (in Yiddish) or *b'rit milah* (in Hebrew). The person who does this procedure is called a *mohel* or *mohelet*. That person is a little bit like a doctor because he or she knows how to do this special procedure safely and carefully, and a little bit like a rabbi because he or she knows all the prayers to say as well. Some *mohels* (*mohalim*) are in fact trained as doctors.

Circumcision is an ancient ritual that has been taking place for almost four thousand years in the Jewish community. Other cultures around the world also circumcise their boys. The word *bris* comes from the Hebrew *b'rit*, which means "covenant" or "promise." For Jews, circumcision symbolizes a promise made by God and Abraham in the Book of Genesis. In the Torah, God promises to give the Land of Israel to Abraham's future children, and Abraham promises to worship only God. Ancient people used to cut things to show that they were serious about the promises they made. Circumcision was the symbol of a very serious promise between the Jewish people and God.

When a grown man chooses to become Jewish through conversion, he may have a circumcision if he hasn't already, or he may participate in a ceremony that is like a symbolic circumcision in which a tiny prick is made with a pin to draw a drop of blood. Not all rabbis in the Reform Movement, however, require circumcision for grown men who wish to convert to Judaism.

What is a baby naming?

When a Jewish baby girl is given her Hebrew name, this ceremony is often called *b'rit hachayim*, "the covenant of life," or *b'rit bat*, "covenant of the daughter." This ceremony may take place on the eighth day of a child's life or when a little girl is one month old. There is no one right time to hold this ceremony. Some families wait until their daughter is almost one year old. At this service, the parents explain why they picked their daughter's name, and prayers and blessings are said that wish for a great life in which the little girl will grow up to be a person who does good deeds, studies, and finds love. Her parents pray that her name will make her happy and that she will be a good person who helps the Jewish people and all people in the world.

A Jew might have an English name or a French name or a Spanish name that she or he uses every day. But all Jews can have a Hebrew name. For Jews whose relatives came from the eastern part of Europe (Ashkenazic Jews), these Hebrew names often are the same as or similar to the names of a person in the family who has died. Sometimes a name with the same meaning is given, or a name that starts with the same first letter. This is a lovely way to keep the memory of someone alive. It is a tradition for Jews from Arab countries or of Spanish descent (Sephardic Jews) to name children in honor of relatives who are still alive. This is a beautiful way to honor special relatives. A Hebrew name has two parts. The first part is the actual name. The second part says that a person is the "son of" or "daughter of" his or her parents. For example, a boy named David whose parents' Hebrew names are Yaakov and Devorah will be called David ben Yaakov v'Devorah, which means David, son of Yaakov and Devorah. Often, Hebrew names are the names of people in the Bible or the names of beautiful flowers, parts of nature, or places in the Land of Israel. When a Jew is called up to chant the blessing over reading the Torah, his or her Hebrew name is used. At a Jewish wedding, a bride and groom sign their Jewish marriage contract (*ketubah*) with their Hebrew names. When Jewish people die, the rabbi uses their Hebrew name in the prayers at the funeral, and their Hebrew name is often written on their tombstones. Having a Hebrew name is an important part of being Jewish.

What is consecration?

Consecration is a special ritual or custom that welcomes children into the formal study of Judaism at their synagogues. In many synagogues, the consecration ceremony takes place around the time of the holiday of Simchat Torah, the Jewish holiday that celebrates the study and reading of the Torah scroll. Children who are just beginning religious school often are called up for a special blessing on the bimah in front of the open ark. Learning and study are important values in Judaism. When parents promise to teach their children about being Jewish and start them on the road of Jewish learning, it is a time for happiness and celebration.

In English, "consecration" means "to be devoted to something" or "to make something very special, sacred, holy." When we learn about being Jewish, we become able to be more sacred and holy in our lives.

What is a bar or bat mitzvah?

When a Jewish child turns thirteen years old, he or she is considered to be a Jewish grown-up in certain ways. The boy is called a bar mitzvah and a girl is called a bat mitzvah when they turn thirteen years old and one day (although there is also a tradition of considering a girl to be a bat mitzvah when she is twelve years old and one day). When children reach this status of becoming a bar or bat mitzvah, it does not mean that they are grown up in the sense of being old enough to get married or go to college. Rather, Jewish tradition believes that people who have reached the age of bar or bat mitzvah are now responsible for fulfilling the mitzvot, or commandments, found in the Torah. This means that instead of parents making all your Jewish choices for you, once you become a bar or bat mitzvah you have to start making Jewish choices for yourself. Part of becoming a bar or bat mitzvah also means that you are ready to do more to help other people in your community and in the world. A bar or bat mitzvah is now ready to learn even more about what it means to be Jewish, how Jews pray, and what Jews have believed and thought about over the years.

Each synagogue celebrates bar and bat mitzvah a little bit differently. It is customary for a boy or girl to be called up to the Torah to say a blessing over the reading of the Torah as part of becoming a bar or bat mitzvah. In some temples, boys and girls help lead a Shabbat service. They may read or sing some of the prayers, chant from the Torah, read or chant from the Prophets (haftarah), and give a short speech (*d'var Torah*) about some of their ideas about the Torah reading. Sometimes the bar or bat mitzvah leads the service by himself or herself. At some synagogues, two or three young people have their celebration on the same day and lead the service together.

Many years ago, when boys reached the age of thirteen, there would be a small celebration when it was time for the boy to begin doing the mitzvot in the Torah. About seven hundred years ago, the ritual of the boy being called up to chant the blessing over the Torah began. In 1921, a young woman named Judith Kaplan recited the blessing over the Torah reading, read from the Torah portion for that week (even though she read out of a book and not the Torah scroll itself), and recited the blessing after reading from the Torah. She became the first girl to celebrate becoming a bat mitzvah in a public way in America.

Many young people celebrate this achievement with a party for family and friends. It is also a wonderful time for families to help others and share their happiness by giving *tzedakah* to people in need. When some boys and girls become a bar and bat mitzvah, they look outside of their own homes and think about the fact that they are part of a bigger family of people, who may need their help. In honor of becoming a bar or bat mitzvah, many young people do a special project, sometimes called a mitzvah project or a *chesed* project. In Hebrew, *chesed* means "kindness." Being kind to others is an important way of showing that you are growing up. These projects might involve volunteering at a local animal shelter, running a book drive for an after-school center, helping to clean up a local park, or raising money for a children's hospital. There are many ways that young people can make a difference in the lives of others.

What is confirmation?

Confirmation is a ceremony held at the synagogue for students in high school. Most students undergo confirmation sometime between tenth and twelfth grade. After becoming a bar or bat mitzvah, students can still attend religious school and increase their knowledge about Judaism. The ceremony is called confirmation because these students "confirm" their ongoing connection to Judaism. Confirmation usually happens during the springtime around the Jewish festival of Shavuot, the holiday that celebrates the giving of the Torah to the Jewish people and the Jewish people's promise of making the Torah an important part of their lives.

Reform Jews started the practice of confirmation about two hundred years ago in Europe. Reform Jewish boys did not always celebrate becoming a bar mitzvah. Instead, students would study in religious school and then, at the age of thirteen, "confirm" their faith together in a confirmation ceremony. Later on, girls were confirmed also. As families continued to hold bar mitzvah celebrations, confirmation began to take place at an age later than thirteen. Today, confirmation is a way to continue Jewish studies beyond becoming a bar or bat mitzvah and to remain connected to the synagogue, the rabbi, the cantor, and fellow students.

What is conversion?

Some people are born Jewish. Other people become Jewish through a process called conversion. There are several steps involved in conversion. After reading many books about Judaism, going to synagogue, celebrating the Jewish holidays, and studying with a rabbi, the person participates in a ceremony and officially becomes Jewish. In the time of the Bible, being Jewish was considered to be passed on from fathers to their children. In more recent times, being Jewish was considered to be passed on from mothers to children, from one generation to the next. In the last thirty years, Reform Jews have decided that if either your mother or your father is Jewish, and you celebrate Jewish holidays and participate in Jewish life-cycle events (like having a baby naming or becoming a bar mitzvah), and learn about being Jewish, you are considered Jewish.

Anyone may choose to be Jewish if he or she decides, after a great deal of thinking and studying, that this is the right thing to do. He or she studies with a rabbi and takes a class with other people learning about Judaism. Then the person meets with three knowledgeable Jews (called a *beit din*, or court), answers some interesting Jewish questions, and discusses his or her ideas about being Jewish. Some rabbis require that the person has a special ceremony in which he or she goes to a ritual bath (*mikveh*) and dips in the warm, clean water three times and says a blessing. The person may also pick a Hebrew name and have a special ceremony similar to when a Jewish baby is born. It is important to think seriously about whether or not becoming Jewish is the right choice, and in most cases rabbis require that someone be an adult or at least a teenager before taking this step.

People who convert to Judaism are considered to be just as Jewish as people who are born Jewish. All people who convert are called Jews. But some people also use the expression "Jews-by-choice" to refer to those who have made that decision. Many years ago it was considered bad manners to even bring up the fact that a person had chosen Judaism. In fact, Judaism teaches that a convert shouldn't be made to feel different from any other Jew. In the thinking of the ancient Rabbis, though, people who convert to Judaism are considered to be some of the dearest members of the Jewish community (*Midrash Tanchuma*). In the Bible, the Book of Ruth teaches us about a righteous convert who showed great *chesed*, or kindness, to her mother-in-law. Ruth became the great-grandmother of King David. Later in Jewish history, there were people who were born into different religious faiths but who converted to Judaism and even became famous rabbis.

What is a Jewish wedding?

When people get married, they have a ceremony called a wedding. At their wedding, they promise to help one another be the best people they can. They also promise to love, honor, and take care of each other. A Jewish wedding service has two main parts. The first part is called *kiddushin* or *eirusin*, and it announces that this bride and groom have chosen to get married to each other. They have a unique relationship that they do not have with anyone else. The second part is called *nisuin* and contains seven traditional wedding blessings.

The Jewish wedding has some special parts that make it a little different than other weddings. Here are some of the important parts of a Jewish wedding:

- Jewish weddings happen on certain dates on the Jewish calendar. Jewish weddings do not take place on Shabbat, which is a day of rest, or on other Jewish festivals.
- At a Jewish wedding, the bride and groom, along with some of their family members, usually stand under a canopy called a chuppah. The chuppah has four poles, and it is a symbol of the home the couple will make together.
- Usually there are at least ten adult Jews (a minyan) present at a Jewish wedding.
- A Jewish marriage contract, called a *ketubah*, is signed before the wedding. The *ketubah* can be written in Hebrew, Aramaic, or any other language spoken by the couple getting married. It is often decorated with beautiful drawings or paper-cut images. The *ketubah* contains promises the bride and groom make to one another. A minimum of two Jewish witnesses sign their names on it; generally the bride and groom sign as well, as does the rabbi or cantor who will help with the wedding. The *ketubah* or parts of it are read during the wedding.
- Rings are exchanged, and the groom and the bride say a special sentence in Hebrew and English that officially marries the couple. They say, "Behold, you are consecrated to me with this ring, according to the law of Moses and Israel."
- The *Sheva B'rachot*, or Seven Wedding Blessings, are read or sung. These seven blessings include the blessing over wine,

thanks to God, and hope for happiness for the new couple.

- A glass, wrapped carefully in a napkin or special bag, is stepped on and broken by the groom. In some cases the bride also breaks the glass. This custom teaches us that even in our happiest moments, we need to remember that some things in the world are still broken. We also recall the beautiful Temple that once stood in Jerusalem and that life became broken in many ways for our ancestors when it was destroyed. This helps to show the couple that as a Jewish family, it is their job to do what they can to make the world a little bit better.
- Everyone says *mazal tov*, or "congratulations," to the bride and groom after the glass is broken.
- A celebration takes place where friends and family can visit with one another and eat and dance.

Even though everyone hopes that the bride and groom will always stay together, sometimes married people decide that they cannot always be husband and wife. Judaism allows people to get divorced. If Jews get divorced, they can go to a rabbi and have something called a *get*, a Jewish divorce decree, which says that according to Jewish law, they are no longer married to each other.

What happens when someone Jewish dies?

Everything that is alive will die someday. Everything that breathes, eats, or moves will one day stop breathing, eating, and moving. We hope that the people we care about will live long lives filled with good health and many happy times and days. We don't want the people we love to ever go away from us. But the world works in its own way, and death is a part of the process of being alive.

Many helpful customs and traditions have arisen over time to aid us when someone we love dies. These customs help when we are sad, and they help people who care about us give us comfort.

When someone is dying, it is very kind to keep that person company so that he or she will not feel lonely. We can talk to them, sing to them, or even just hold their hand. If they are well enough to speak, they might enjoy having a conversation. Jewish tradition teaches us it is good to say we're sorry for anything bad that we might have done. This is true at the end of someone's life as well. If a person thinks that he or she will not live very much longer, it is a good time to say sorry. Judaism has a ritual for this last apology, called *vidui*, or confession. In addition to saying sorry, the person may recite the *Sh'ma* prayer: "Hear, O Israel, the Eternal is our God, the Eternal is One!"

Judaism teaches us that it is important to care for the dead, even though they cannot thank us or even know that we are helping them. Our tradition gives us many ways to care for them and show them proper respect, from the moment they die until they are buried. When the person dies, the body is covered with a sheet, and the people around it say, *"Dayan ha-emet,"* which means "Judge of truth." This reminds us that we are given our lives by God, and that life is a precious gift. A person, called a *shomeir*, or "guard," stays with the body until it is put into a box called a casket and then, at the funeral, into the earth. The job of taking care of the dead person's body goes to a group of people from a funeral home or a *chevrah kadishah*, a group of volunteers from the Jewish community who help take care of the dead. They make sure that the body is clean, and they say special prayers or psalms from the Bible. These people show deep respect for the body of the person who has died and demonstrate much kindness by helping with this difficult job.

Sometimes, if someone very close to us in our family dies, we put a small, cut black ribbon onto our clothes at the time of the funeral. Some people put a little rip or tear in their clothes. Both of these actions are a symbol of how we feel at that time. It is like our life has been torn and is no longer whole.

A funeral is the service that takes place after someone has died. It can be held in a synagogue or a funeral home or at the cemetery. Some prayers and psalms, poems from the Bible, are recited to help comfort the family and friends. The rabbi or family members or friends speak about the person who has died in a talk called a *hespeid*, or "eulogy." Sometimes they tell funny stories about the person or try to remember the good things that made that person a mensch, a decent human being. A prayer called *El Malei Rachamim* (God Is Full of Compassion) is chanted.

At the cemetery, where the bodies of dead people are buried, the body is carried in a casket from a special car called a hearse. The casket is carried to the grave, the space in the ground where the person will be buried. After the casket goes into the grave, the *Kaddish* prayer, which speaks about the holiness of life, is recited by the mourners. Then the mourners help fill the grave with dirt. Helping to bury the body of the person they loved may seem strange, but Judaism teaches that this is another way to show respect to the dead. In this way, we make sure that our loved one has a fitting burial place.

Most Jews are buried in the ground. Some choose to have a cremation, although it is not something that traditional Jewish law permits. Cremation is when a person's dead body is turned into ashes. These ashes can be buried, kept in an urn, or spread out in the wind or over some water.

After the *Kaddish* prayer is said at the cemetery, people form two lines for the mourners to walk between, as a symbol of support in their difficult time. Friends and relatives tell the mourners, "May God comfort you among all the mourners of Zion and Jerusalem." Then the family members go back home, where they observe a custom called *shivah.*

Shivah comes from the Hebrew word *shevah*, which means "seven." *Shivah* describes the seven days that close relatives stay at home to mourn. For seven days they spend a great deal of time thinking and talking about their deceased loved one. They light a candle that burns for seven days. During the time of shivah, it is a Jewish custom for friends to visit the mourners. This is called "paying a shivah call" or "making a shivah visit." It is not like a regular visit to someone's house, when you are the guest and they are the hosts. When you make a shivah call, you don't even knock on the door or ring the doorbell, but you go right into the house, so that you don't bother the mourners. Visitors give a hug or express words of comfort to someone who is crying. It is customary to bring food so that the mourners won't have to worry about cooking meals during that week. Visitors also come to help make up a minyan for one of the prayer services in which *Kaddish* is traditionally recited. If the mourners want to talk, visitors also come ready to listen to stories about the person who has died and to share memories. In all these ways, mourners are helped to feel comforted, cared for, and reassured that they are not alone in their sorrow.

In some communities, people sit shivah for only three days and then slowly begin to participate again in their everyday activities. The Talmud describes the first three days after a funeral as a very intense time of mourning or sadness. During the four days following that period, the mourning may not be quite so intense. Whether or not people observe shivah for three days or seven days, the main idea is that friends and loved ones help take care of one another during difficult times in each other's lives.

What happens after we die?

No one knows for certain what happens to us after we die. Different people have different ideas about life after death. Throughout Jewish history, rabbis have borrowed ideas about life after death from the different cultures and religions around them and made these ideas into Jewish ones.

Some rabbis said that after good people die, the souls or spirits that live inside their bodies fly up to heaven and have a wonderful time forever and ever. They go to a place called *olam haba*, "the world-to-come," or *Gan Eden*, "the Garden of Eden." There is no pain in this heavenly place. The rabbis imagined that in this perfect world-to-come, a Jew can study Torah all day long. Since this was their favorite activity, you might understand why this would have been their version of a perfect world. The rabbis of the Mishnah and Talmud taught that one day in the future, when the world will become a perfect place, all of the dead people will live again. At that time, all the Jews will live together in the Land of Israel.

Today, many Jews believe that after we die, our souls live on through the good things that we did when we were alive. There is a famous saying that the deeds of righteous people are their memorials. We remember those people who have died by the kind way they acted while they lived and by their words and ideas. People can live on after their bodies die by the good work they did, by the charity they gave, and by the values they passed on to their children, grandchildren, students, and other people they loved.

Knowledge gained from the modern study of science has also influenced the way some Jews think about life after death. Some people believe that our bodies are constantly changing and are made up of matter created by God. The tiny atoms that make up our bodies may have come from fragments of stars a very, very long time ago. When we die, this matter becomes different kinds of energy. Ultimately, the matter (or stuff) in our bodies turns into the matter that makes up stars and flowers and other things in this universe. In this way, we remain connected to the living world even after we die.

Some Jews believe in an idea known in Hebrew as *gilgul hanefesh*, or reincarnation. Literally, *gilgul hanefesh* means "the rolling of the soul," and though this is not a common Jewish belief, some Jewish thinkers have believed that the soul lives on after death and moves from one body to another.

Since we cannot say for sure what happens to us after we die, we can work hard to treasure our lives and value the time that we have. It may make people feel better to think that after death, good people are rewarded for their actions, and bad people suffer for their evil deeds. But we don't know if this really happens or not. For now, all we know for certain is that the Torah teaches us to "choose life" and to make each day a blessing by our actions. What matters is how we live our lives here and now.

Resources for Further Reading on the Jewish Life Cycle

BOOKS FOR ADULTS

Choosing a Jewish Life: A Handbook for for People Converting to Judaism and Their Family and Friends, by Anita Diamant. Schocken Books, 1998.
Choosing Judaism, rev. ed., by Lydia Kukoff. URJ Press, 2005.
The Jewish Baby Handbook: A Guide for Expectant Parents, by Douglas Weber and Jessica Brodsky Weber. Behrman House Publishing, 1990.
The Jewish Home, rev. ed., by Daniel B. Syme. URJ Press, 2004.

The Jewish Mourner's Handbook, by William Cutter. Behrman House Publishing, 1992.

Jewish Views of the Afterlife, by Simcha Paul Raphael. Jason Aronson, 1996.

The New Jewish Baby Book: Names, Ceremonies, & Customs: A Guide for Today's Families, 2nd ed., by Anita Diamant. Jewish Lights Publishing, 2005.

The New Jewish Wedding, rev. ed., by Anita Diamant. Scribner's, 2001.

The New Name Dictionary: Modern English and Hebrew Names, by Alfred J. Kolatch. Jonathan David Publishers, 1984.

On the Doorposts of Your House: Prayers and Ceremonies for the Jewish Home, edited by Chaim Stern with Donna Berman, Edward Graham, and H. Leonard Poller. CCAR Press, 1994.

A Time to Mourn, A Time to Comfort: A Guide to Jewish Bereavement and Comfort, by Ron Wolfson. Jewish Lights Publishing, 1995.

What Happens After I Die? Jewish Views of Life After Death, by Rifat Sonsino and Daniel B. Syme. URJ Press, 1990.

BOOKS FOR CHILDREN

Bar/Bat Mitzvah Basics: A Practical Family Guide to Coming of Age Together, edited by Helen Leneman. Jewish Lights Publishing, 1996.

A Candle for Grandpa: A Guide to the Jewish Funeral for Children and Parents, by David Techner and Judith Hirt-Manheimer. UAHC Press, 1993.

For Kids—Putting God on Your Guest List: How to Claim the Spiritual Meaning of Your Bar or Bat Mitzvah, by Jeffrey K. Salkin. Jewish Lights Publishing, 1998.

When a Grandparent Dies: A Kid's Own Remembering Workbook for Dealing with Shiva and the Year Beyond, by Nechama Liss-Levinson. Jewish Lights Publishing, 1995.

Chapter 4

THE BIBLE

- Are the Torah and the Bible the same thing?
- Who wrote the Bible?
- Are the stories in the Torah and the Bible true?
- Why do we read the same stories over and over?
- What will happen if I break one of the Ten Commandments?
- Why should I try to be like the people in the Torah when they were not always so great?

The questions in this chapter tend to elicit all sorts of discomfort for a modern Jewish parent or educator. Outside of a traditional setting, these questions compel us not only to take a hard look at the Torah, but also at our entire Jewish identities. If we do not believe that the Torah is the word of God, then we are presented with a potentially slippery slope of questions regarding faith and the fulfillment of ritual commandments. Who are we as Jews? What do we believe? If the Torah is a document of human artistry, how can it still be sacred for us and our families?

Once, at Temple Shaaray Tefila, a fifth-grade religious-school teacher asked me to speak with his class. The students had been studying the biblical Patriarchs (Abraham, Isaac, and Jacob) and the Matriarchs (Sarah, Rebekah, Rachel, and Leah). In the midst of their text studies, the students had unanimously concluded that the figure of Jacob was a terrible disappointment to them. Jacob played a dirty trick on his twin brother, Esau, conspired with his mother to deceive his father, and ultimately played favorites with his own children. Therefore, this sensitive class of ten-year-olds decided that Jacob's name should be removed from the list of patriarchs in the *Avot V'Imahot* prayer of the *Amidah* (the heart of the prayer service). The teacher was stunned. As the school principal and a rabbi at the synagogue, I was both eager and a bit anxious to speak with this group of students. We discussed the narratives in the Torah and explored the concept of midrash and how rabbis had defended or criticized figures from the Torah by filling in gaps in the stories and creating other scenarios about these same characters. We spoke about the meaning of Jewish prayer and about Jacob's struggle to find God and to find his own true identity. While respecting the students' beliefs about Jacob's actions, we sought to find a way to keep this class's prayers united with those of the greater Jewish community.

A few important lessons came out of this interaction with our forefather Jacob. I learned that it was all right to agree with the students that Jacob was not all good. They were able to understand that because of his stature and also because of his struggles, Jacob should remain in the honor roll of patriarchs. Despite his personal failings, Jacob did transmit Judaism to his children. He did sincerely struggle with God and try to understand what God wanted from him. We agreed that we could learn from Jacob because of his deeds, both good and bad.

The discussion with this class of intelligent fifth graders was not one of serving as a defense attorney for Jacob, arguing against the prosecution. Rather, we sat together and discussed our beliefs about what it means to be a good child, sibling, and parent. In fact, arguing about how to interpret our sacred texts is an age-old Jewish tradition. It was a wonderful opportunity to engage in passionate discourse on belief, God, and Jewish history with this group of students. Our discomfort with this story and an ancient prayer led to a discussion and a reinforcement of values for all involved.

Our Rabbis taught us that human beings struggle with two wills or instincts, *yetzer hara*, the "bad impulse," and *yetzer hatov*, the "good impulse." It is our goal to improve the world by acting on the *yetzer hatov* that exists in all of us. Developing a relationship with the stories and characters in our Bible can help us fine-tune our own positive impulses. Let your children voice their discomfort with some of what they learn about in our texts, and use their comments as opportunities for debate, discussion, and further engagement with the texts. Just as the friction that an oyster experiences helps it to form a pearl, so too can the uncomfortable discussions and tensions that arise from our religious struggles result in something beautiful and precious.

✦ ✦ ✦

Are the Torah and the Bible the same thing?

The Torah is one part of the Hebrew Bible. *Torah* is a Hebrew word that means "teaching" or "instruction." The Torah is the scroll made

up of parchment and wooden rollers on which the first five books of
the Bible are written. The Torah is written by hand in Hebrew by a
person called a scribe. The Torah is also sometimes called the Five
Books of Moses. These five books are the first books of the Bible. In
book form, the Torah is called a *Chumash*, from the Hebrew word
chameish, which means "five."

The Torah contains five different books. Each book has a
Hebrew name and an English name. Their names are *B'reishit*—
Genesis; *Sh'mot*—Exodus; *Vayikra*—Leviticus; *B'midbar*—Numbers;
D'varim—Deuteronomy. The Hebrew names come from one of
the first words of each book. The English names come originally
from Greek or Latin. Each book tells part of the story of the Jewish
people.

The word "Bible" comes from a Greek word that means "books."
There are thirty-nine books in our Bible, although different religions
count the books slightly differently. Our Bible is sometimes called
the Hebrew Bible or Hebrew Scriptures. In Hebrew, our Bible is
called the *Tanach*. The *Tanach* is made up of three sections, and the
word *Tanach* comes from the first letters of these three different sections. The *T* in *Tanach* is a *tav*, the first letter in the word *Torah*. The
N is a *nun*, for *N'vi-im*. The *Ch* is the *kaf*, from the word *K'tuvim*.
Christians refer to our Bible as the Old Testament, though Jews
don't use that name.

N'vi-im are the books of the Prophets. They form the second part
of the Bible. The prophets were people who told the Israelites to
behave properly and act in kind and decent ways. The prophets told
the Israelites not to bow down to idols or statues. The prophets told
the Israelites to take care of people who didn't have much money.
The early prophets lived around the time of King David, around
1000 B.C.E. The last prophets lived about the time when the

Babylonians destroyed the Temple in Jerusalem, around 586 B.C.E. The books of the Prophets include Joshua, Judges, I and II Samuel, I and II Kings, Isaiah, Jeremiah, Ezekiel, Hosea, Joel, Amos, Obadiah, Jonah, Micah, Nahum, Habakkuk, Zephaniah, Haggai, Zechariah, and Malachi.

K'tuvim are the books of the Writings. They make up the third section of the Bible. These books are Psalms, Proverbs, Job, Song of Songs, Ruth, Lamentations, Ecclesiastes, Esther, Daniel, Ezra, Nehemiah, and I and II Chronicles.

The word "Torah" can also have a much broader meaning than just the Five Books of Moses. Jews often use "Torah" to mean any kind of Jewish learning. The Torah is our most sacred, most special book. All of our other Jewish books, like the other books in the Bible as well as the Talmud, Mishnah, and midrash, have their roots in the Torah. And because learning is such an important Jewish value, all Jewish learning relates to the Torah in some way.

Who wrote the Bible?

Some Jews believe that God wrote the Torah section of the Bible. These people believe that the words in the Torah are the exact words Moses heard on Mount Sinai from God. God told Moses everything that should be in the Torah, and Moses wrote it in his own handwriting. Then, the words of the Torah were passed down from generation to generation. In synagogue, when we finish reading from the Torah scroll and hold it up for everyone in the congregation to see, we sing, "This is the Torah that Moses placed before the people of Israel, according to the word of God and the hand of Moses."

Some Jews believe that the Torah did not come straight from God. They believe that different people heard stories that had been passed on through the ages and continued to share these important lessons. Eventually, these stories were written down and put together by a few people. The people who edited or pasted these stories together did this work with a deep sense of respect for God and the laws in the Bible. They were doing holy work when they put these stories in a book. According to this way of thinking, people wrote the Torah, inspired by God.

Some of the books of the Writings section of the Bible, like the Book of Ecclesiastes, are thought to have been written by King Solomon. Some people say that King David wrote Psalms. The books of the Prophets are supposed to be the actual words of those prophets. Yet many of the people who study the Bible do not think that these kings or prophets were the actual authors of these books. Perhaps some of the parts of those books were actually written by the prophets mentioned. We do not know for certain. We do know that the *Tanach* is read by many people around the world and that people have changed the way they live their lives because they have read the Bible and taken its stories and lessons into their hearts.

Are the stories in the Torah and the Bible true?

Children, and adults too, often want to know whether or not the stories in the Torah and the rest of the Bible are true. Was there a huge flood like the one we read about in the story of Noah and his ark? Did Sarah really have a baby when she was over ninety years old? Did the Nile really turn into a river of blood? Did manna really drop down from the heavens six days a week while the Children of Israel were wandering in the wilderness? Was Moses's head really surrounded by rays of light?

One of the reasons we ask these questions is that we are trying to understand the importance of the Bible. If the stories are not true, we might think they have no value to us. Maybe they are just for fun, like television shows or storybooks. What makes this book more special than other books? Why should we care about these stories?

The Bible is a collection of the stories that Jewish people believe are precious and important enough to save—not only as a part of our history, but also because of lessons and ideas in the stories. The Bible can teach us many important lessons about life and the way human beings should treat one another and our world. It is not a science textbook, though. Many Jews today do not believe that the world was literally created in six days or that frogs actually jumped on Pharaoh's nose as part of a punishment for refusing to let the Israelites go free. But whether or not the story of Creation really happened as it is described in the Bible does not make the creation of the world any less of a miracle. The ways that living creatures breathe, the way that the seasons change, and the way that the stars seem to twinkle in the sky are all wonders of Creation that we celebrate each Shabbat and in our prayers.

Even if not one frog ever hopped on Pharaoh's sandals or the banks of the Nile three thousand years ago, the story of the Exodus is still very powerful for the Jewish people. The events may not have happened exactly the way the story tells us, but the ideas in the story of Passover remind us that having freedom is an important part of being human. The experience of the Israelites in the desert also teaches us how hard it can be, but how important it is, to be part of a people. These are both absolute truths.

We do know that the lessons in our Torah are worthwhile. Even if they are a bit like myths, or stories that have been passed on from generation to generation and been changed along the way, we know that we can learn about the meaning of a greater "truth" when we study them. Our Rabbis taught that when a person learns Torah, he or she has everything that is really important. It says in the Talmud: "Once a person acquires knowledge, what does that one lack? But if a person does not acquire knowledge, what does that person possess?" (Babylonian Talmud: *N'darim* 41a). The Rabbis believed that learning makes us strong and wise. Being wise means much more than knowing facts. Being wise means knowing *ideas* that are true, even if facts are not one hundred percent precise.

Why do we read the same stories over and over?

Every week at synagogue, we read a portion of the Torah. There is one portion for each week of the year. At the end of the year, we finish all five books of Torah and celebrate at a festival called Simchat Torah (Rejoicing in the Torah). At Simchat Torah services, we read the end of the last book of the Torah, Deuteronomy, and begin reading the very first verses of Genesis. Every single year, we start reading the Torah and finish reading the Torah, only to begin again.

When there are so many important Jewish books to read, you might wonder why we read the same stories over and over. We do so because we never stop finding new wisdom and learning in the Torah. When we listen to the story of Jacob and Esau, the twins who struggled with each other, we hear it differently depending on who we are. When we are children, we may think about how Jacob or Esau were feeling when Jacob convinced Esau to sell him his birthright and gained all the privileges of being considered the firstborn son. When we hear this story again when we are older, we may think about why Rebekah, their mother, favored one son over the other and helped her son trick her husband. We may question why Isaac was unable to give equal blessings to his two sons. We may think about the way we treat our own brothers and sisters now that we are grown-up. The stories in the Torah grow up with us, and we are able to see different parts of them as we hear them over and over.

You may enjoy hearing the same stories or watching the same movies over and over again. This is one way that human beings learn. When we hear the Torah stories over and over again, we learn new ideas and discover new lessons each time, even though we may have heard the same words before.

A rabbi named Ben Bag Bag used to say about the Torah, "Turn it, and turn it, for everything is in it. Reflect on it and grow old and gray with it. Don't turn from it, for nothing is better than it" (*Pirkei Avot* 5:22). Other rabbis in the Talmud explained that the Torah is so rich with information and lessons that it takes many years to learn from it. They wrote: "Why is the Torah compared to the fig tree? The fruit of most trees, the olive tree, the vine, and the palm tree, is collected all at once, while that of the fig is collected a bit at a time. So, too, regarding the Torah: today a person learns a little, and tomorrow we shall learn much, for the Torah cannot be learned in a single year or two" (Babylonian Talmud, *Eiruvin* 54a).

One of our responsibilities as Jews is to keep teaching the stories in the Torah to future generations. Your parents and teachers transmit it to you, and you in turn can transmit it someday to another generation. In this way, we keep our connection to the Torah and to Jewish history and tradition active and alive. Each time we hear, read, or teach a story from the Torah, we learn something new from it.

What will happen if I break one of the Ten Commandments?

The Ten Commandments (*Aseret HaDibrot* in Hebrew) are found two times in the Torah. The first time they appear is in Chapter 20 of Exodus, and then we find them again in Chapter 5 of Deuteronomy. In the Torah, the Ten Commandments are said to be "revealed" or given to the Israelites. This moment is a powerful one because, according to the Rabbis, it shows the love that God has for the Israelites in providing them with laws. The giving of the Ten Commandments in the Torah is a covenant, or an agreement, made between the Israelites and God. The Israelites choose to follow God's law after God saves them from being slaves. They make this choice as free people, willingly.

Today, more than three thousand years later, Jewish people around the world read the Ten Commandments (or the "Decalogue") in the Torah portions of *Yitro* and *Va-et'chanan* and at the springtime festival of Shavuot. In order to show respect for the importance of these rules, it is a custom to stand up in synagogue when the Ten Commandments are chanted or read aloud.

Some Jews believe that these commandments were created by human beings rather than God. If a person accepts that these rules were not necessarily given by God, then there is some room for choice, although almost everyone would agree that the basic rules like "do not murder" should be followed. Other Jews believe that a significant part of being Jewish is following all the commandments as closely as possible. Either way, it is important to examine these rules closely as you grow older to discover why they have been so precious to the Jewish people. As you learn more about the commandments, you can think about how you believe you should respond to them.

Many of the rules in the Ten Commandments are basic guidelines that, when followed, help all people in the world live together peacefully. For example, the commandments teach us not to murder or steal. If you break one of those commandments, you are also breaking a law of the country in which you live, and there will be consequences like paying a fine or going to jail. Lying about what someone did (being a false witness) is also a crime. Even if no one knows that you broke a commandment, it has an effect on your heart and in your mind. One of the commandments teaches us not to "covet," which means not to want something that belongs to someone else. You will not go to jail for coveting your friend's house, puppy, toy, clothes, computer game, or bicycle. But you are changed for the worse when you covet and focus energy on being jealous. Breaking a commandment hurts other people and damages us as well. It takes away a part of what makes us human. Breaking a commandment separates us from our community and destroys relationships.

The fourth commandment teaches us to remember the Sabbath day and keep it holy. It is up to us to decide exactly how we do this. When we make Shabbat a beautiful part of our week in some way, we can make our lives richer, longer, and filled with deeper meaning. There are many different ways that we can keep this commandment. For some people it might be having Shabbat dinner together with their family. For others it might be going to synagogue and not working at all on Shabbat. For still others, it might mean doing something special, like taking a walk or a hike. Part of our job as Jews is figuring out what it means to us personally to keep a commandment.

As we grow up, we learn that some rules, like wearing a seat belt, exist so that we do not hurt ourselves or other people. Some rules, like going to school, help us make our lives more productive and useful. The Ten Commandments fulfill both of these functions. Some of these rules are based on laws from other civilizations or governments that came before the Jewish people. All people in the world need rules so that human beings can live together peacefully. The Ten Commandments are more than just a regular set of rules though, because they teach us about Shabbat and about our relationship with God. When we take these commandments to heart and act on them, we can help make our homes and our society work more smoothly.

There are actually many more than just ten commandments in the Torah. The Rabbis from many years ago taught that there are a total of 613 commandments. Some of these commandments, or mitzvot, tell us how to behave with each other. They teach us to act in good and decent ways and take care of those who need our help. Other commandments are rules about what we should eat or how we should celebrate holidays. Not every Jew believes that these kinds of rules are still important. It is valuable to study these ancient traditions and discover how they have influenced the Jewish people over time. Being familiar with them can make us feel part of the larger community of Jews around the world. When you study about Judaism, you learn more and more about the many different commandments, not only the Ten Commandments.

Why should I try to be like the people in the Torah when they were not always so great?

Sometimes we are told that we should try to copy the values and virtues of our ancestors from the stories in the Torah, particularly those of our Patriarchs and Matriarchs: Abraham, Isaac, Jacob, Sarah, Rebekah, Rachel, and Leah. Yet, when we get older and actually take a closer look at some of the stories in the Torah, we learn some interesting and sometimes upsetting things about these figures. Because he is afraid that he might get hurt, Abraham lies to an Egyptian king. Isaac would give only one special blessing to one son, even though he had two children. Jacob, with Rebekah's help, tricked his father in order to take the special rights of the older child. These are our first Jewish "heroes," and it is sometimes disappointing to learn about their faults. Why should we try to be like these people when they made mistakes and hurt themselves and others?

Our Torah is special because it allows us to view our ancestors from a perspective that is not always so complimentary. Our forefathers and mothers were not perfect. Human beings often must struggle to live up to their highest selves. We learn so much about human nature and behavior when we study about the struggles and mistakes of some of our heroes in the Bible. We can try to focus on their positive attributes and integrate those behaviors into our lives, and we can learn from their mistakes. Abraham was a hospitable and noble person who was brave enough to believe in one God when others had a different way of looking at life. Isaac was famous for being a loving and good husband. Jacob was clever and able to make peace with his brother after his struggles. When we can look at the people in our Bible and admit that they were not superheroes, we can learn how they continued to grow even after they were grown-ups. We can be inspired to keep trying to be our best versions of ourselves. We can learn that it is never too late to learn to do better.

Resources for Further Reading on the Bible

BOOKS FOR ADULTS

Back to the Sources: Reading the Classic Jewish Texts, by Barry W. Holtz. Simon & Schuster, 1986.

Living Torah: Selections from Seven Years of Torat Chayim, edited by Elaine Rose Glickman. URJ Press, 2005.

Stories of Heaven and Earth: Bible Heroes in Contemporary Children's Literature, by Hara Person and Diane Person. Continuum Publishing, 2005.

The Torah: A Modern Commentary, rev. ed., edited by W. Gunther Plaut. URJ Press, 2005.

A Torah Commentary for Our Times, by Harvey J. Fields. UAHC Press, 1993.

Who Wrote the Bible?, by Richard Elliot Friedman. HarperSanFrancisco, 1997.

The Women's Torah Commentary: New Insights from Women Rabbis on the 54 Weekly Torah Portions, edited by Elyse Goldstein. Jewish Lights Publishing, 2000.

BOOKS FOR CHILDREN

Be Not Far from Me: Legends from the Bible, by Eric Kimmel. Simon and Schuster, 1998.

Children's Bible Stories from Genesis to Daniel, by Miriam Chaikin, illustrated by Yvonne Gilbert. Dial Books, 1993.

Daughters of Fire: Heroines of the Bible, by Fran Manushkin, illustrated by Uri Shulevitz. Harcourt, 2001.

The First Book of Jewish Bible Stories, by Mary Hoffman. DK Publishing, 2002.

Sefer Ha-Aggadah: The Book of Legends for Young Readers, by Seymour Rossel. UAHC Press, 1996.

Stories from the Bible, by Lisbeth Zwerger. North-South Books, 2000.

Tommie dePaola's Book of the Old Testament, by Tommie dePaola. G. P. Putnam's Sons, 1990.

Who Knows Ten?, by Molly Cone. UAHC Press, 1998.

Chapter 5

ISRAEL

- What is Israel?
- Where is the Land of Israel?
- Have Jews always lived in Israel?
- Is everyone in Israel Jewish?
- Why should I feel connected to Israel?
- Why should I visit Israel?
- Why is there fighting in Israel?

How can we sing a song of the Eternal on foreign soil?
If I forget you, O Jerusalem, let my right hand wither;
let my tongue cleave to my palate if I cease to think of you,
if I do not keep Jerusalem in memory even at my happiest hour.

—Psalm 137:4–6

While studying in rabbinical school, I was invited to attend a luncheon with a group of visiting Israeli business, political, and educational leaders. Of the fifteen participants, two were missing their right arms. Without asking them if they had lost their arms due to accidents or illnesses, I automatically assumed that their present condition resulted from their mandatory service in the Israeli armed forces. One man was the mayor of an Israeli city, and the other served as an educator for a large youth movement. At the meeting, these two individuals discussed not only their professions, but also their goals for the State of Israel.

After the lunch meeting, the image of those two Israelis remained in my mind. I reflected on my own identity as an American Jew and my responsibilities toward the land and people of Israel. The words to Psalm 137 came to my mind: "If I forget you, O Jerusalem, let my right hand wither." If anyone at that table was guilty of "forsaking" Jerusalem, was it not one of the American Jews sitting there? How bitterly ironic that the Israelis, whose lives have been shaped so profoundly by the precept of not forgetting Jerusalem, were the ones missing limbs!

As Jews, how do we understand our relationship with the land and people of Israel? The meeting that day stayed with me, perhaps in part because I was left with many unanswered questions. Because I am a Jew, should I reside in the Jewish homeland, in the Land of Israel? Would my making *aliyah*, moving to Israel, fulfill me as a human being, as a Jew? Would I help to fulfill a vision of the "Jewish mission" by living in Israel? And if I do not, must I feel ashamed for not choosing to live in a certain geographical location? Should I feel more connected to an Israeli stranger than a British one simply because of my religion and shared history? What responsibilities do I feel toward Israel? How can I teach my children or students to feel connected to Israel? How can I feel connected when I don't always agree with what Israel does?

These questions have been confronting Jews since the first exile over two thousand years ago. From the biblical to the Talmudic periods as well as medieval and modern ages, Jews have expressed their positions on this topic. For some, a Jew has an obligation to live in the sacred land of *Eretz Yisrael,* the Land of Israel, in order to live most completely as a Jew and to fulfill the human side of the covenant between God and the Jewish people. Conversely, others believe that it was precisely the interface between Jews and their non-Jewish surroundings in the Diaspora that created the dynamism and creativity of the Jewish religion. For the early Reformers, a Jew's homeland was the country in which he or she was born or chose to immigrate to, not necessarily the Land of Israel.

Jewish parents and educators today are in the position of addressing these questions and conveying a sense of our complex relationship with Israel. We can talk to our children about Israel. We can tell them that Israel is a vibrant center of Jewish culture and tradition. We can tell them that Israel is the ancient homeland of the Jewish people and provides meaningful opportunities for Jewish self-expression. We can share with them experiences of celebrating the Jewish calendar as a daily, national calendar and of living on streets named for the heroes and scholars and poets of our own people. If we want our children to feel connected to Israel, there must be some sort of relationship between our children and the land and people of Israel—visits to Israel; experiences with Israeli music, art, and literature; and studies in Hebrew language. No one can truly love what he or she has not encountered. The people of Israel are our family. As with family, we can sometimes disagree while still loving and supporting each other. We can all learn from one another and be enriched by these family ties.

What is Israel?

Israel is a country in the Middle East, located above Africa on the east coast of the Mediterranean Sea. Israel takes its name from the biblical patriarch Jacob. In the Bible, Jacob's name changes to Israel. Later, the land where Jacob's (who is also called Israel) family lived was known as the "Land of Israel." The people who lived in Israel in biblical times were called Israelites. Today, people who live in Israel are called Israelis.

More than five million Jewish people live in Israel. The modern State of Israel, which is what the country is called, was founded on May 14, 1948. But the idea of the Land of Israel as a homeland for the Jewish people has existed for nearly four thousand years. During its history, the land currently known as the State of Israel has been called by many names, including *Eretz Yisrael* (Hebrew for "Land of Israel"), Canaan, Zion, Palestine, the Promised Land, and the Holy Land.

Where is the Land of Israel?

Israel is located in the Middle East. Israel is very small; it is about the size and shape of the state of New Jersey. On its west are the shores of the Mediterranean Sea. It lies north of the African continent and to the west of Asia, while it is just south of Lebanon, Turkey, and the countries in Europe. It is completely surrounded by the Mediterranean Sea and the Arab countries of Lebanon, Syria, Jordan, and Egypt. The country is 10,840 square miles in size. It is 290 miles long and 85 miles across at its widest point and not even 8 miles wide at its narrowest point. If you are flying in an airplane to Israel from New York, you can arrive there in less than twelve hours.

Have Jews always lived in Israel?

Jews have lived in Israel since the time of Abraham. In the Book of Genesis in the Torah, we read that Abraham purchased land in this area of the world and that Abraham made a promise, or covenant, with God. In the twelfth chapter of Genesis, God tells Abraham to move to "the land that I will show you, I will make of you a great nation, and I will bless you." At that time, this area was known as the land of Canaan.

When there was a famine, a shortage of food, in the land, Abraham's great-grandchildren settled in Egypt, where there was plenty of food. These people from Canaan who lived in Egypt became known as the Children of Israel because their ancestor was Jacob, also known as Israel. After the Exodus from Egypt, the Children of Israel conquered the land of Canaan from the Canaanites and other tribes living there. Later, King Saul became the first king of the twelve tribes of Israel and helped the Children of Israel fight against their enemies, including the Philistines. After Saul was king, King David took over. His son, King Solomon, brought together the tribes who lived in both the northern and southern parts of the land. King Solomon built a beautiful Temple in Jerusalem. The Ark of the Covenant was placed in this Temple; musicians sang there, and people traveled three times a year during the time of the Pilgrimage Festivals to give offerings at the Temple. After King Solomon died, the tribes who lived in the north decided to have their own kingdom, which was called Israel. The two tribes in the south called themselves Judah. In 722 B.C.E., the kingdom of Israel was attacked by the Assyrians, and the people were thrown out of their homes. These ten tribes of Israel disappeared, leaving only the kingdom of Judah. Then, in 586 B.C.E., the Judeans were removed by force from their land by the Babylonians. The memory of the Land of Israel stayed in the hearts and minds of the Jews for years and years.

The Judeans brought the Torah, the writings of the prophets, and other sacred words with them to Babylonia, where the country of Iraq is today. Generations later, when the Jews were allowed to return home, some hurried back as soon as they were permitted. Other Jews had found that they could lead happy lives in countries outside of the Land of Israel and stayed where they were. Whenever countries like Persia or Rome took control of Israel, some Jews continued to live there, while other Jews moved to different countries.

Just fifty years after the Babylonian exile, King Cyrus of Persia gained control of the part of Israel called Judea. In about 536 B.C.E., Cyrus allowed the Jews to return and rebuild the Temple in Jerusalem. This time in Israel's history is often called the period of the Second Temple.

About two hundred years later, in 312 B.C.E., the Greeks gained control of this area of the world from the Persians. The Syrians then gained control of Judea after the death of the leader of the Greeks, Alexander the Great. The story of Chanukah, in which the the Maccabees fought against the Syrians for the right to live their lives freely as Jews in Israel, took place 166–137 B.C.E.

A dark time in Jewish history happened when the Romans conquered the Land of Israel. Taking away the rights of the Jews, the Romans destroyed the Second Temple and killed many Jews in the year 70 C.E. In 135 C.E., the Romans destroyed Jerusalem, exiled more Jews throughout the Roman Empire, and sold thousands of Jews into slavery.

After this time, the Jews were not allowed to come into Jerusalem unless given permission by the different empires that had control of their land. Persians invaded Palestine in 614. Then the Byzantines took over in 629. In 650, Moslems built a sacred mosque in the middle of Jerusalem, right on the spot where the First and Second Temples had once stood.

Control of the Land of Israel, and the ability of Jews to return there to live, changed many times over the next two thousand years. Christians from Europe spent four hundred years trying to take Israel from the Moslems in a series of wars called the Crusades, which began around 1095. As these soldiers made their way through Europe on their way to Israel for the purpose of making the land a place for Christians only, they killed many of the Jews they met along the way. In 1291, the Moslems regained control of the land from the Crusaders. In 1492, Jews were made to leave their homes in Spain, where they had earlier been welcomed. Some of these Jews were able to move back to the Land of Israel. By 1517, control of Israel changed yet again when the Ottoman Turks took over. Then in 1799, Napoleon's French army took over towns in Palestine, but after just a few months, his army left. This began a period of time in which European countries became interested in having control over the Land of Israel.

Two hundred years ago, some Jews from Europe began to think more and more about leaving the countries where they were living. Jews in Europe had to cope with laws that made life very difficult for them, and their lives were often in danger. Some Jews began to think about moving to Israel, at this time called Palestine, as a way to live freely and safely as Jews. This way of thinking about returning to live in Israel was called Zionism. These Jews from around the world who moved to Palestine were called pioneers, or *chalutzim*. Some Jews formed groups to prepare to move to Palestine and make the desert a homeland, where they could grow food and build homes. They wanted a state of their own where they could live in safety.

One of the first people to put these ideas into words was a Jewish writer from Austria named Theodor Herzl. In 1896, he published a book called *The Jewish State*, in which he explained that the Jewish people should be permitted to create their own state in the Land of Israel. People who agreed with these ideas were called Zionists. Herzl was a reporter covering the story of Alfred Dreyfus, a captain in the French army who had been accused of treason, giving secret information to France's enemies. Herzl found out that the reason why people were accusing Dreyfus, who was in fact innocent, was because he was Jewish. During his trial, the crowd yelled out, "Death to the Jews." All of this made Herzl very angry. He started to believe that Jews needed a homeland of their own, where they could be full citizens and accepted completely.

Herzl's work helped turn the Zionist dream into a reality. In 1948, after much struggle against those who did not want the Jews to have their own country, Israel became an independent Jewish state. Israel's Declaration of Independence says: "The Land of Israel was the birthplace of the Jewish people. Here their spiritual, religious and national identity was formed. Here they achieved independence and created a culture of national and universal significance. Here they wrote and gave the Bible to the world. In recent decades they returned in masses. They reclaimed the wilderness, revived their language, built cities and villages and established a vigorous and ever-growing community with its own economic and cultural life." This means that Israel has always been an important place for Jewish people and that Jewish people have a right to call Israel their home.

Is everyone in Israel Jewish?

Although most people who live in Israel are Jewish, not everyone in Israel is Jewish. There are about 6.5 million people living in Israel as citizens. More than 5 million of those people are Jewish. According to the Israeli Ministry of Foreign Affairs, most of the remaining million and a half individuals are Arab Moslems or Arab Christians. There are also Israelis who belong to the Druze religion, who live mostly in the north of the country. There are small groups of other religions as well.

Even the Jews in Israel come from a wide range of backgrounds. Jews from all over the world call Israel their home. In Israel there are Jewish immigrants from Ethiopia, Vietnam, China, Russia, Poland, Sweden, South America, South Africa, and India, as well as the United States and Canada.

Why should I feel connected to Israel?

Israel is where some of the most important events in Jewish history took place. Many of the stories in the Bible happened in the Land of Israel. Israel is the land promised to our ancestors in the Torah. The two Temples that were the center of Jewish life were in Israel. Israel is the place where the Jewish religion began, changed, and grew. Even if we don't live in Israel, it is our Jewish home.

During all the years that Jews couldn't live there, Israel remained in the hearts and minds and prayers of the Jewish people. Jews didn't forget about Israel when they lived in other countries, and many Jews continued to hope that they would be able to return to the Land of Israel one day. One way to see how Jews have felt connected to Israel no matter where they lived in the world is to look at a prayer book. We have prayers that ask that God bless the land and the people who live in Israel. Some of the blessings in our prayer book even change when the seasons change in Israel. When fall begins, Jews across the globe pray for rain to help the crops grow in Israel. Some prayers even mention a hope that one day the city of Jerusalem will be rebuilt the way it was thousands of years ago during the time of King Solomon, and that when this happens there will be true peace in the world.

Jews have stayed connected to Israel in other ways as well. During Jewish weddings, the rabbi or cantor chants a prayer asking that the cities of Israel and streets of Jerusalem always be filled with sounds of joy and happiness. Many Jews send *tzedakah* to Israel to help plant trees, feed the poor, or build hospitals. There are many schools, colleges, and programs in Israel in which people can study about Judaism, Hebrew, and nonreligious subjects as well. Every day, Jewish people from around the world "make *aliyah*," or move to Israel to make it their home.

Today we are lucky to live in a time and place when, as Jews, we are allowed to live where we want, study what we want, marry whom we want, work at what we want, and practice our religion in the way we want. We are comfortable living in the United States or in Canada, or in many other countries around the world. We are accepted and welcomed and have the same rights as all citizens. We are at home wherever we live in the world. But this has not always been the case for Jews. Even if we don't choose to live in Israel, having a Jewish country makes all Jews safer and prouder.

There is a saying in Hebrew: *Kol Yisrael aravin zeh bazeh*. This means that all Jews are united, linked, and bound together. We are connected to each other through our shared history, our prayers, our customs, and our beliefs. *K'lal Yisrael* is an expression that means "all Jewish people." As a Jewish person, you are not alone. You have a family that includes more people than just your relatives. You are a part of *K'lal Yisrael*. All Jews—your parents, your grandparents, the Jews in your family, your synagogue, your city— are part of your extended family. As a Jewish person, you have family across the world. Being connected to Israel is part of being connected to this larger family. Israel is a foreign country on the other side of the world, but it is also the Jewish homeland that Jews have dreamed of for centuries.

Why should I visit Israel?

Do you visit your grandparents, cousins, aunts, or uncles during the year? Families that like to stay connected try to visit one another frequently. When you visit your relatives, you may exchange stories, see how everyone is, and celebrate important family occasions together. Jewish people often visit Israel for similar reasons. As Jews, much of our history happened in the Land of Israel. Jews from all over the world visit Israel to make a connection with the land and the people. They may study Judaism, the Hebrew language, or even other subjects while they are there. They may go on tours of famous places mentioned in the Bible and hike around the mountains, lakes, and valleys of the land. Some Jews enjoy visiting Israel during Jewish holidays; they experience what it feels like to celebrate Rosh HaShanah, Yom Kippur, or Passover with an entire country. When a Jew visits Israel, it is often very different than visiting other countries. Visiting Israel is a little bit like getting to know a member of the family.

A visit to Israel has the ability to change you in powerful ways. A Jew visiting Israel realizes that all of the stories learned in religious school, all of the holiday customs from home, and all of the Hebrew words or expressions that she or he might know are more than individual pieces of knowledge. All of these pieces come together when visiting Israel. Being in a Hebrew-speaking country, walking on streets in which the trees and rocks have witnessed so much history, seeing the many, many different Jewish ways to live makes you think more deeply about Judaism and become more connected to your Jewish history. This kind of deep reflection makes being Jewish more important and makes you think more about what being Jewish can mean in your life in the future. When many Jews visit Israel for the very first time, they often say that they have a sense of feeling at home. Israel is the homeland for Jews. Wherever a Jew may live on this planet, he or she has another home in Israel.

Why is there fighting in Israel?

The official emblem, or picture, of Israel is a menorah with an olive branch on each side of it. The olive branch is a symbol of peace. Peace has always been an important Jewish value. Our prayer book is filled with prayers for peace. Anytime Jews pray together, some of what we pray for is peace. Israel's goal has always been to achieve a lasting peace with its neighbors and all countries.

Because of where Israel is located, throughout history many countries and peoples have wanted to have control of it. Imagine that your home was designed so that your bedroom was the most convenient passageway between the kitchen and the rest of the house. Everyone in your home would always be trying to go through your room in order to get a snack or to go to the front door. The people in your home would want to pass freely through your room. They might even want to take your room as their own in order to be able to move around more easily whenever they felt like it without having to ask your permission.

When Israel was first being settled by the Hebrew tribes thousands of years ago, it experienced this exact problem. Different nations like the Assyrians, Babylonians, or Romans wanted to control Israel so that they could bring their armies and navies into other parts of the world much more easily. They also wanted to be able to trade more easily with other countries.

Today, the people who live in Israel are no longer fighting those ancient empires. For the past hundred years or so, the major challenge to living in peace has come from neighbors in the Arab countries that surround Israel. There has been a great deal of fighting between the Jews in Israel and some of the Arab nations living in that area of the world. According to the Bible, the Jews trace their roots to *Eretz Yisrael*, the Land of Israel, from the time of Abraham and Sarah, and their son, Isaac. In the Torah, God tells Abraham that he should move from his homeland to the Land of Israel, then called Canaan, and that his descendants would inherit this land. But the Torah also teaches that Abraham had another son too. His name was Ishmael, and he was also given some land in this area. Ishmael came to be thought of as the father of the Arab people. The Jews came from the children of Isaac, and the Arabs came from the children of Ishmael. Jews and Arabs can say that they have the same great-great-great-great-great. . . grandfather, Abraham. We are cousins. And yet we both believe very powerfully that the land belongs to only us. For a more detailed history of the situation, see the appendix.

Despite many good efforts, such as the Oslo Accords of 1993, no real overall peace has yet been achieved. Attacks on Israel and on Israelis have continued. There are terrorist organizations, like one called Hamas (which means "violence"), that do not recognize the right of Israel to exist in peace and security. They do not want to work out an agreement with the government of Israel. They want the Arabs living in Israel to have their own state without any Jews in it. For Hamas and other similar groups, one of the main goals is to hurt any Jews living in Israel. Terrorist attacks have hurt and killed innocent people on city buses and streets, in pizza restaurants, at colleges, at Passover seders, and in hotels. When these attacks occur, the Israeli army often fights back and tries to capture or hurt more terrorists. Sometimes innocent Arabs are hurt or killed when this happens.

The situation in Israel is complicated. Both Jews and Arabs have reasons to want the land and to believe that it belongs to them. Jews have a very long history of connection to the Land of Israel, going back to the stories in the Torah. After a long history of having to move from country to country throughout the centuries without ever having a real home, Jews are proud and relieved to have Israel as our homeland. At the same time, many Arabs believe that Israel is an Arab homeland too, called Palestine.

Israel is trying to deal with these problems in many different ways. In 2004, the Israeli government started to build a fence between areas where many Arabs live and places where many Jewish people live. At the same time, certain areas were turned over to the Palestinians so that they could rule themselves there and wouldn't have to live under Israeli control. Hopefully in the future, Israel, the Palestinians, and the Arab countries around her will be able to work out a solution to this very difficult situation. Perhaps one day soon there will be true *shalom*, peace.

Resources for Further Reading on Israel

BOOKS FOR ADULTS

Exodus, by Leon Uris. Bantam, reissued in 1983.
A History of Israel: From the Rise of Zionism to Our Time, 2nd ed., by Howard M. Sachar. Knopf, 1996.
Walking the Bible: A Journey by Land through the Five Books of Moses, by Bruce Feiler. Perennial, 2002.

BOOKS FOR CHILDREN

Come, Let Us Be Joyful! The Story of Hava Nagila, by Fran Manushkin. UAHC
   Press, 2000.
Jeremiah's Promise, by Kenneth Roseman. UAHC Press, 2002.
Joshua's Dream: A Journey to the Land of Israel, by Sheila F. Segal. UAHC
   Press, 1992.
Our Land of Israel, by Chaya M. Burstein. UAHC Press, 1995.
*Walking the Bible (Children's Edition): An Illustrated Journey for Kids through
   the Greatest Stories Ever Told*, by Bruce Feiler. HarperCollins, 2004.

Chapter 6

ANTI-SEMITISM

- Why do some people dislike Jews?
- What was the Holocaust?
- What should I do if someone says something bad about Jews or Judaism?

We dream of our children inhabiting a world in which they are enveloped in love, kindness, and acceptance. Yet even in the most enlightened societies of the twenty-first century, some of our children may encounter bigotry or anti-Semitism in one of its many forms. How do we teach them to feel proud of their Jewish identities without teaching them to feel superior to those from different backgrounds and faiths? How do we help them learn to stand up for themselves without falling into a cycle of creating more physical or verbal violence? How do we help them understand the reasons for anti-Semitism and not feel ashamed of being Jewish? In addition, how do we model understanding and acceptance of differences for others without losing our unique religious heritage?

A mother in my synagogue spoke to me about her second grader, a delightful little girl, who enjoyed coming to religious school. The child had learned some facts about the Holocaust and had been told that Jewish people had been hurt and killed by the Nazis. The little girl announced that she would now like to become another religion, since people hated Jews. She asked her mother: "What new religion should the family select?"

How would you handle this situation? How do we, as parents, share the often difficult story of the Jewish people without driving our children away from Judaism? How do we balance the real suffering that Jews have endured with the equally real joys of Jewish life, holidays, and achievements?

These are not easy questions. Yet we take a step forward when we answer sensitively and in ways that are appropriate for our children's development. Gingerly, we can present a balanced approach in our explanation of the travails that Jews have endured, as well as the glorious aspects of Jewish history. Presenting Jewish history solely as a litany of offenses and wars against an embattled people gives our children a distorted view of Jewish life. Inviting them to see themselves as part of a tribe of victims who have been hated for centuries instills only a sense of anger and helplessness and will do little to inculcate a sense of love and curious wonder for Jewish living. Instead, teaching our children how Jews have continued to persevere and create a dynamic and lively religion even in the face of difficult circumstances is an ennobling lesson.

In 1939, my mother-in-law was a little girl fleeing Germany on the ship St. Louis. The journey of this ship came to be known as "the voyage of the damned." The majority of the nine hundred passengers were Jews escaping Nazi Germany for safe harbor in Cuba. Yet the visas and landing certificates that they had purchased were not accepted when the passengers reached their destination. In spite of their visas, their ability to sustain themselves financially, and the death sentence hanging over their heads back in Europe, the Cuban government refused to admit these Jews. At that time the United States had become resistant to accepting Jewish immigrants and would not accept these passengers. The non-Jewish captain tried to delay sailing back to Germany. He knew what would happen to his passengers back in Europe. Finally, four countries, France, Belgium, England, and the Netherlands, agreed to host the passengers. My mother-in-law's family found temporary refuge in Brussels, Belgium. There, she attended kindergarten while her mother struggled to find a means to escape from Europe. Nearly a year after their ship returned to Europe, in April of 1940, my mother-in-law and her mother were able to board a ship to the United States. My mother-in-law barely escaped Hitler's long arm. Her grandparents, who were scheduled to leave on the next ship, were like so many others, not as fortunate. The Nazis invaded Belgium in May of 1940. Her grandparents were murdered in Auschwitz.

My mother-in-law's stories are part of who she is: memories of her father's arrest on *Kristallnacht*, "the Night of Broken Glass"; the firefighters standing by, hosing down the surrounding buildings as her Black Forest village's synagogue was burned; the last look on the faces of her grandparents, whose flight from Europe was forbidden by the Nazis. For years, she kept these stories from her children. She wished to raise proud Jewish sons. Yet, slowly, small fragments of these memories seeped out from their secret places, and they have helped shape her adult children's Jewish identities.

For some of our children, their first brush with the idea of anti-Semitism occurs when they learn about the Holocaust. For others, it comes through an encounter at school or camp. Some children today may become concerned about the danger of being Jewish when they hear about the too-frequent bombings of synagogues and Jewish institutions around the world and terrorist attacks on Israelis; or when they need to pass a security check to get into the local Jewish Community Center or when they see armed guards stationed in front of synagogues on the High Holy Days. Certainly, we need to be honest with our children when we share with them the struggles of the Jewish people. Pretending that the world is always fair and kind will not prepare our children for some of the more difficult realities that they may face. We help our children grow strong physically when we inoculate them against the viruses infecting our world. Likewise, at times we need to expose children to disturbing information in order for them to continue to grow emotionally in a healthy manner. It is important to speak about these realities in an honest but balanced way. If we do so with caring, with understanding, and with a strong conviction that we will always protect them to the best of our abilities, we can help our children grow up knowing that life is not perfect, but that we and they can improve it. Much can be done to make the world a better place, not only for Jewish people, but also for others struggling for dignity and equality.

It is true that there are still people in the world who would like to hurt Jews. But remind your child that most people are good and would never want to hurt them. Most people in the world just want to live together peacefully. You can focus on the importance of living in peace with people from all different backgrounds, and learning about and respecting one other.

When your children ask about the horrors perpetrated by Nazis, you can tell your children about the unbelievable sacrifices and acts of kindness displayed by some of the non-Jews who risked their lives to save Jewish friends, colleagues, and even total strangers. These individuals are known as Righteous Gentiles, and their kindness and resistance to evil are stories that need to be told as well. An entire town in France, called Le Chambon sur Lignon, hid many Jews and saved their lives. The king of Denmark refused to adopt anti-Jewish laws even after the Germans occupied that country in 1940, and the Danes smuggled over seven thousand Jews to safety across a fifteen-mile channel of water to Sweden. Righteous Gentiles who had nothing to gain from saving Jewish lives rescued innocent people. There were acts of kindness and gentleness amid the cruelty of the *Shoah,* the Hebrew term for the Holocaust.

If your child is beginning to ask about anti-Semitic slurs, perhaps he or she is experiencing some sort of bias. You may wish to sit down with your child and ask him or her about what is going on. Even very young children understand that sometimes people do bad things and hurt other people. Sometimes no matter what we do to make people like us, they have bad feelings about Jews or other people who are different from them. If a bully is picking on your child because he or she is Jewish, that person may be picking on someone else due to any number of factors (race, religion, etc.). Children need to be reassured that when they share with a caring adult that someone is hurting them, they are not being "tattle-tales." The child who seeks help is protecting him- or herself and possibly other victims of that bully.

Providing your child with a solid understanding of basic Jewish beliefs and customs can offer some of the most powerful protection against intentional and even unintentional verbal slurs by ignorant individuals. Sometimes children are called upon to explain aspects of Judaism to non-Jewish peers or adults. Children may feel uncomfortable when placed in this position of spokesperson for the Jewish religion. Yet it is precisely this role as educator to others that holds the key to unlocking barriers between people of different faiths. The matzah sandwich in your child's lunchbox during Passover, the day of school missed because of Yom Kippur, the invitation to a bar or bat mitzvah celebration that your child's non-Jewish friends receive may all place your child in the position of informal teacher of Judaism.

When I was in high school, I attended a summer program with other teenagers from Virginia. One young man told me that I was the first Jewish person he had ever met. He wondered if I had horns on my head, giving voice to an old superstition. I vividly remember our conversation, as I explained that indeed Jews did not have horns on their heads. I told him that though some people thought Jews had horns, the idea was due to a misunderstanding about the Hebrew word *keren*, which can mean either "ray" or "horn." In the Torah, after Moses speaks with God, Moses is described as having *keren-or*, "rays of glory," shining about his head. This was mistakenly understood by some to mean that he had actual horns growing out of his scalp. Because of my Jewish learning, I was able to engage in a productive dialogue about this image of Jews and horns. A rich Jewish education is an incredibly potent defense against anti-Semitism and a powerful gift for your children in developing a burgeoning sense of self.

Hopefully, the days of showing young people firsthand footage from Nazi death camps without any explanation or background information is a thing of the past. Today, a plethora of thoughtful educational materials and books exist that help us share the tragic stories of anti-Semitism with our children in an age-appropriate manner. We can tell our children with pride that even though some misguided people may not like Jews, we are proud of who we are. We are not going to change our religion because someone does not understand us or like us. Judaism will continue into the future.

There are organizations like the Anti-Defamation League that have existed for almost one hundred years to fight discrimination of any kind. When we support these groups and share with our children that we are not alone in fighting against hatred, we can help replace our children's fear with confidence. When we are examples to our children and fight against prejudice, we continue that glorious mission of *tikkun olam*, the repair of this broken and fragile world.

Why do some people dislike Jews?

Those who study the way humans behave say that people show prejudice and bigotry toward other people when they do not feel good about themselves. Think about someone you know who picks on other people. In order to feel important, some people find it necessary to put other people down and make fun of them, hate them, or even hurt them. They may dislike Jews because they feel unsure about themselves. Like bullies, they look around for people who are different to pick on and hurt.

Some people grow up in homes in which they are taught to dislike those who are different from them. They are taught to dislike and mistrust what they don't know. They may even be told that Jewish people are "bad." They may have been taught lies about Jewish people. Some people falsely believe that Jews were the ones who killed Jesus, who is a very special person for Christians. People who don't like Jews just because they are Jews are called anti-Semites. This word comes from a tribe of people, the offspring of Noah's son Shem, who are thought to be the family that all Jews come from.

Throughout much of history, Jews were not always treated the same way as non-Jews. Sometimes Jews could not hold certain kinds of jobs or own land. They often had jobs that made other people not like them very much, like being tax collectors. Other times, Jews were made to leave certain countries if the king or leader of that country felt like making them go. When Jews were allowed to stay and make a home for themselves, they often had to live in the same crowded neighborhood with other Jews called a ghetto. The gates to the ghetto were locked at night. It was almost impossible for Jews to make friends with people who were not Jewish.

In the Middle Ages (from about 500 to 1500), and even into the 1900s, some people mistakenly believed that Jewish people made matzah for Passover out of the blood of Christian children. This ridiculous accusation is known as the blood libel. This terrible lie made it hard for Jews to live in certain towns in Europe and still continues to cause hatred in some parts of the world today.

Because Jews usually lived close to one another and did not always visit with or socialize with non-Jewish people, it might have been easy for the non-Jews to think of them as very different from themselves. Because they ate foods that were prepared in special ways, according to the laws of keeping kosher, and therefore did not share meals with non-Jews, some non-Jewish people might have felt that Jews were not friendly.

When Jews were allowed to leave the ghetto and make friends with non-Jewish people, some of this distrust of Jews went away. It is easy to be afraid of strangers or things that we do not know about. When someone has ideas about a certain group of people without actually knowing those people, he or she may feel prejudice against them. He or she may be judging before getting to know the person. When people display prejudice, they are showing an ugly side of themselves. They are showing that they are not giving people a fair chance. When people meet each other face-to-face and get to know one another, it becomes clear that all people are basically the same underneath their skin.

Today, there are many people in the world who help to fight hatred and unfairness against Jews and against people of all different colors and religions. As Jews, we must always remind ourselves that all human beings possess sparks of holiness. Each life is precious. The Torah teaches Jews that since we were strangers in the land of Egypt, we should understand how it feels to be different and misunderstood. It is therefore our duty as Jews to look out for the poor, the stranger, and anyone who is considered different. Judaism teaches us not to hate people in our hearts. The Torah instructs us to love our neighbors as we love ourselves. These are commandments that are not always easy to follow. But we can make a huge difference by the small things that we do and say. We can help get rid of hatred by helping people understand each other better and learn not to judge on the basis of religion, color, race, or anything else.

What was the Holocaust?

The Holocaust took place in Europe from 1933 to 1945. The Holocaust was a terrible time in the history of the world and the history of Jewish people. During this time, six million Jews were murdered by the Nazis and their helpers. The word "Holocaust" is translated into Hebrew as *Shoah*, which literally means "complete destruction by fire." Jews remember the Holocaust, or *Shoah*, each year in the springtime on the anniversary of the uprising of the people who lived in the Warsaw Ghetto. The Jewish people in this ghetto fought back as hard as they could against the Nazis. Though they were killed, they showed the world that Jews can stand up for themselves.

During the Holocaust, two out of three Jews in Europe were killed, including one million Jewish children. Adolf Hitler was in charge of the German government before and during World War II. He and his Nazi followers told many lies about the Jews to the German people. After World War I, the people in Germany and some other countries in Europe had a hard time earning a good living. The Nazis told the people that Jews were to blame for these problems. First they took away rights from the Jews. Jews weren't allowed to go to school, they weren't allowed to shop at a store owned by a non-Jew, they weren't allowed to own businesses, and they had to wear yellow Stars of David identifying themselves as Jews. Then the Nazis began to arrest Jews, as well as other people like gypsies and homosexuals, whom they considered to be a bad influence, and put them into horrible places called concentration camps. In the concentration camps, the prisoners were terribly mistreated and sometimes even systematically murdered. Many people in Germany, Austria, Poland, and other parts of Europe and Russia cooperated to murder Jewish people. The Holocaust was a horrendous time in the history of the world.

Many Jews in Europe thought that Hitler would lose his power and that the laws that were made to hurt them would be changed. But Hitler stayed in power, and the people in charge of the government made it almost impossible for Jews to run away to other countries after the Nazis took over. Even when Jews were able to leave Germany, there were very few places in the world where they could go. Many countries that would have been safe places for Jews had rules about how many Jews could come in. Jews were turned away from many countries, including the United States. The modern State of Israel was under the control of the British at that time and was called Palestine. The British would not let very many Jews come to Palestine either. Because they couldn't find another place to go, Jews were trapped in Europe during the Holocaust.

The Jews in Europe suffered and many died because of the anti-Semitic actions of the Nazis and their supporters. Although there were some good people in Germany, and other places like Denmark, who chose to assist the Jews and saved lives, many people did not care or bother to help those in need. They were not necessarily Nazis or anti-Semites; they simply chose not to do anything. One of the lessons we learn from the Holocaust is that when people do not speak up for other people, terrible things can happen. Sometimes being silent can be as terrible as actually doing something, because instead of stepping in to help, your silence lets someone else get hurt.

Martin Niemöller was a Protestant minister in Germany who spent over eight years in a Nazi concentration camp. Even though he was not Jewish, he ended up suffering during the Holocaust. More than five million people who were not Jews died in the Holocaust along with the six million Jews who were killed. Niemöller wrote that when one group of people is treated badly, everyone is affected for the worse. We must not keep silent when other people are suffering from injustice—even if those other people are not our own friends or relatives.

We will never know how much the world lost because of the Holocaust. Perhaps one of the people who died in the Holocaust would have found a cure for a terrible disease, composed a beautiful piece of music, or written an incredible book. So many people never had a chance to grow up or enjoy their lives because of the

Holocaust. Jewish people across the world have promised that we will "never again" allow another Holocaust to take place. We must work hard to make sure that people of all countries are safe from the pain and destruction caused by hatred.

What should I do if someone says something bad about Jews or Judaism?

If someone says something bad about Jews or Judaism, or calls you a bad name, your first reaction may be to get upset. You may wish to call the person a bad name right back or even hit the person. Sometimes, people show parts of themselves that are not courageous. They may feel jealous or hurt or angry at you for any number of reasons. Instead of talking about why they are really mad, they may end up saying something cruel about your religion.

If someone calls you bad names because you are Jewish, you may want to treat him or her in the way that you might treat any bully, by telling that person that it's not okay to use that name. When you tell the person that he or she is saying cruel things that are not true, you can show this person that hatred is not okay. It can be scary to deal with a bully or someone who frightens other people just to feel more powerful. Some experts say that you can deal with people like this by trying to change the topic of the bully's conversation. You may feel safer if you stay close to a group of friends when this bully is around. Chances are that you are not the only one being picked on by this person. It is important to speak with an adult who can assist you, like a parent, teacher, or rabbi.

At times children are afraid to tell adults that someone is hurting them. They may not want their classmates to think they are "tattletales." But if someone is calling you a bad name because you are

Jewish, or for any other reason, you need to tell an adult—your teacher, your parent, your rabbi, someone you trust. That adult can help give you ideas for handling the problem, be supportive of you, or even get involved by working with your class to make things better for everyone. Sometimes being courageous means not using our strength or power to hurt someone with our hands, but using our strength and power to tell an adult what is happening so that a bad thing will stop.

The town of Billings, Montana, worked together as a community to show that hatred was not welcome there. During the season of Chanukah in the early 1990s, some Jewish families were showing their Chanukah menorahs in their windows. Some people who did not like Jews decided to vandalize or damage these Jewish homes. When neighbors of the Jews heard about this sad event, they decided to pull together as a community. Suddenly, everyone in the town, Jew and non-Jew, had a menorah in the window. They came together to help fight against hatred. People should be able to celebrate their religion and customs in peace. When the people of Billings, Montana talked to one another about the problem of prejudice and worked together, they were able to tell everyone that caring was stronger than hatred.

Resources for Further Reading on Anti-Semitism

BOOKS FOR ADULTS

The Bully, the Bullied, and the Bystander: From Preschool to High School—How Parents and Teachers Can Help Break the Cycle of Violence, by Barbara Coloroso. Harper Resource, 2004.

The Holocaust: The World and the Jews, 1933–1945, by Seymour Rossel. Behrman House Publishing, 1992.

A Holocaust Reader, by Lucy S. Dawidowicz. Behrman House Publishing, 1976.

Out of the Whirlwind: A Reader of Holocaust Literature, rev. ed., by Albert Friedlander. UAHC Press, 1999.

BOOKS FOR CHILDREN

Anne Frank: The Diary of a Young Girl, by Anne Frank. Bantam Books, 1993.

Escape from the Holocaust, by Kenneth Roseman. UAHC Press, 1985.

The Number on My Grandfather's Arm, by David A. Adler. UAHC Press, 1987.

Rooftop Secrets and Other Stories of Anti-Semitism, by Lawrence Bush with commentaries by Albert Vorspan. UAHC Press, 1986.

The Tattooed Torah, by Marvell Ginsburg. UAHC Press, 1983.

Terrible Things: An Allegory of the Holocaust, by Eve Bunting, illustrated by Stephen Gammel. Jewish Publication Society, 1989.

Chapter 7

JEWISH DIVERSITY

- What is a Jewish family?
- What do Jews look like?
- What makes someone a good Jew?
- Does a Jewish family have to have one mother and one father?
- Why do some Jews dress differently than we do?
- Is every synagogue the same?

This final chapter addresses your children's questions about why Jewish people are a diverse group. I have heard Judaism compared to a tapestry woven from varied threads representing the multitude of Jewish communities and the varied expressions of Jewish living. Your child is one thread in that tapestry. Many colors, fabrics, and designs fill this piece of art. By displaying the patience and motivation to examine this tapestry with your child, you provide a legacy of loving memories, ennobling rituals, and ethical precepts to pass on through the generations.

My mother had a mantra that she repeated to the children in my family over and over: "We don't have to do what other people do. We do what our family does, and we try to do the right thing for us." This answer could be a response to almost any conversation or request for a new toy or outfit or privilege. Sometimes this answer was not what we wanted to hear. Yet that value gave me confidence when facing pressure from acquaintances to engage in behaviors with which I wasn't comfortable. It gave the children in my family the confidence to be different.

For centuries, Jews have not always done what other people do. Even under difficult circumstances, Jews have created a dynamic response to life, leading to the development of rituals, customs, prayers, and behaviors that are sometimes different than what is practiced by others around us. Jews have historically seen ourselves as all connected to one another, a worldwide community with shared values, practices, and concerns, including the responsibility to take care of each other.

Yet despite this level of interconnectedness, not all Jews look alike physically or practice Judaism the same way. When we are young, we may think that all Jews resemble the children in our religious school classes or our cousin's bat mitzvah family photo. But in reality, due to both historic and economic truths, Jews have been dispersed across the globe for several thousands of years. As Jews interacted with the residents of their new homelands, they developed regional gene pools, special languages such as Yiddish or Ladino, unique cuisines and customs, and new ways of responding to Jewish laws and texts. A Jew from India most likely looks very different than a Jew from Poland, or from Ethiopia. And while a Jew from Russia eats matzah along with sweet gefilte fish at the Passover seder, a Jew from Morocco eats his matzah with fish in a spicy red sauce.

Rabbi Joe Forman, my older brother, has a picturesque way of describing the different approaches to Judaism adopted by various denominations or streams within our global Jewish family. "Jews," he explains, "are like an orange. There are sections within Judaism. In those sections are unique individuals. Yet all of the Jewish individuals represented by the segments of the orange are connected in profound ways. There is something in that orange, and in Judaism, that holds us all together."

Rabbi Eliezer taught, "Let your neighbor's honor be as dear to you as your own" (*Pirkei Avot* 2:10). When we are able to recognize the beauty in the diversity of our people, we show *kavod*, or "honor," to our fellow Jews. It may be easy to dismiss those Jews who seem to observe less than we do and label them as somehow "less Jewish" than we are. Likewise, there may be those among us who feel that Jews who observe more than we do exhibit the traits of religious fanatics. Not every Jew is Jewish in exactly the same way that we are. Not every Jew looks like us. Not every Jew celebrates or believes the same way we do. When we acknowledge and honor our differences, we are able to be a whole and healthy family and true, caring neighbors. We may not do exactly the same things that other people do, but our family makes important decisions with care and respect for our Jewish heritage and our special family customs as well.

✦ ✦ ✦

What is a Jewish family?

There is no single snapshot of a "Jewish family" that represents all Jewish families. Jewish families are different. They come from different places around the world. Some Jewish families have their roots in countries in Eastern Europe like Russia, Poland, or Germany. These are called Ashkenazic Jews. Most Jewish people who live in the United States are Ashkenazic. These Jewish families may have physical traits that resemble people from the countries in Eastern Europe. They are often white, with fair skin.

Some Jews are Sephardic. This word comes from the Hebrew word for Spain. Sephardic Jews are descendants of the Jews who were expelled from Spain and Portugal in 1492. These Jews then moved to countries in North Africa, like Morocco or Egypt, or the Middle East. Jews from Iran or Iraq and other Arab countries are also considered Sephardic, even though they might not actually have their origins in Spain. Jews from these parts of the world tend to have darker or even black skin and features. Their families may look like non-Jewish families from Yemen or Morocco.

Some Jews don't have Jewish roots at all. They have converted from other faiths and ethnic backgrounds. They may look like people from Ireland, China, or Kenya, but they have chosen to be Jewish. They may have different ways of saying the Hebrew prayers or different holiday customs. Some Jews were adopted by Jewish families when they were little. These Jews may have been born in such places as Vietnam, Thailand, or Mexico. They may look different from you and your family. Yet, they too are part of our bigger Jewish family.

The State of Israel invites Jews from all across the world to make Israel their homeland and place of residence. Israel is the home to many kinds of Jewish families from all over the globe.

What do Jews look like?

Judaism is not only a religion, a way of looking at life and behaving, but also a rich culture. Judaism is not a race. There are Jews from all races in the world. Although most Jews you have met are probably Caucasian (people with white skin), there are many Jews in the world who have black skin. Some people of African descent convert to Judaism or choose to become Jewish. In Uganda, a country in Africa, there is a community of Jews. There is also an entire community of Jewish people from the country of Ethiopia in Africa. These Jews are often said to be the descendants of King Solomon and the Queen of Sheba. Called *Beta Yisrael*, or "the House of Israel," these Jews have also been called Falashas (which means "stranger"). In the 1980s, twenty-five thousand Jews from Ethiopia were rescued from a famine and were flown to Israel, where they started new lives. This airlift was called "Operation Moses," and these Jews are now part of Israeli society.

Jews may not all be members of the same race or even live in the same country. But all Jews are members of what is called "the people-hood of Israel." In Hebrew, this idea is known as *K'lal Yisrael*. This means that everyone who is Jewish is part of the same extended family. We are all connected in some way to Jacob in the Bible, whose name was changed to Israel. All Jews, no matter the color of their skin or whether they live in Tel Aviv or Tallahassee or Timbuktu, are connected to one another in powerful ways. We may have different ways of honoring Shabbat and different prayers that we recite in synagogue. We may eat different foods and speak different languages. But we are connected to one another because we are a Jewish family. We value the idea that in spite of our many differences, Jews are a "people" and a group who care for one another and help to care for each other.

What makes someone a good Jew?

For many people, being a good Jew means following the moral or ethical rules of the Torah and the teachings of the prophets. The prophet Isaiah said that the most important thing we can do is help the hungry and the poor and create a more just world. Other Jews believe that the right way to live a Jewish life is to follow the many commandments that are the basis for Jewish law. Still other Jews believe that we should focus on the commandments and customs that are personally meaningful for us, celebrating Jewish holidays and life-cycle moments in Jewish ways.

According to Jewish tradition, there are 613 mitzvot, or "commandments," in the Torah. The Talmud discusses many other laws and rules to help us follow these mitzvot. Books such as the *Shulchan Aruch* have been written to provide codes of additional laws as well. These laws are sometimes described as a "fence around the Torah." Just as a fence protects something enclosed inside it, these laws protect the commandments. If a person follows these expanded laws of the Talmud, it won't be possible to even get close to breaking a law in the Torah.

Some Jews believe that the correct Jewish way to behave means following all of the laws that have come down to us over time. For Jews who strictly follow halachah (Jewish law), behaving Jewishly means praying three times each day, saying blessings before and after eating, taking part in certain activities, wearing a *kippah* or head covering to remember God, only eating food that is considered ritually fit (kosher), wearing certain types of clothing to help remember the commandments (such as the *tallit katan*, which is a long piece of cloth with fringes on its corners, worn under clothes), and observing the many commandments in the Torah.

At certain times in history, Jewish people did not have the choice of whether or not to keep many of the traditional rules and customs. Today, our society is more accepting of differences in ideas and practices. The Reform Movement teaches that we do not have to follow all of the Jewish laws in order to be Jews. Reform Jews believe that Jewish laws were created by human beings in order to create a just society. Because times change, not all of the traditional Jewish laws may be important for us to follow today. New customs and new practices have been created that make our Judaism meaningful to us today. Not following a Jewish law does not make us bad Jews or bad people. We are still Jews even if we practice Judaism differently than our friends or relatives.

Trying to label ourselves or others as "good Jews" or "bad Jews" is not a very helpful activity. Regardless of the level of our observance, we are all Jews. Perhaps it is a better use of our energy to try to improve our world or even learn more about Judaism, so that we may understand this tradition, find meaning in its rules and customs, and live more fully as Jews.

Does a Jewish family have to have one mother and one father?

No, a Jewish family does not have to have one mother and one father. There are many different kinds of families. Some children live with aunts, uncles, or grandparents. Some children are raised by two mothers or two fathers. Other children have only one parent. Jewish families are not all the same. What is important is how people in families treat one another. The Torah teaches us to respect our parents and honor them. The Hebrew word for "parents," *horim,* comes from the same root in Hebrew as "teacher," *moreh* or *morah,* and Torah. Honoring those who guide us with wisdom and love is an enduring Jewish value that has been part of Jewish families for generations.

Why do some Jews dress differently than we do?

Jews come from many different countries and cultures around the world. These Jews may dress in ways that are typical of the people in their countries. Some male Jews from Arab countries cover their heads with kaffiyehs, the head wraps usually associated with Arabs.

Though today most Jews dress like their non-Jewish friends and neighbors, there are Jewish customs regarding dress and clothes that have come down to us over the centuries. A concept called *tz'niut* means "modesty in dress and behavior." It is a Jewish value to dress with a sense of respect for one's body and not display oneself to the world. How a person interprets *tz'niut* varies from one Jewish community to the next.

Chasidic Jews appeared in the 1700s in Eastern Europe. The word, "chasidic" comes from the Hebrew word *chasid*, which refers to a person who is pious or strict in religious behavior. These groups were originally known for devoting energy to joyful prayer and honoring the righteousness found in the lives of ordinary people, not just in rabbis and scholars. Today, there are different Chasidic communities. Chasidic Jews still believe in the importance of regular prayer and strict observance of Jewish laws under the leadership of their rabbis. They also place a great deal of emphasis on study and meditation. Though there are Chasidic Jews throughout the world, there are large Chasidic communities in North America, particularly in Brooklyn, New York, and in Europe and Israel. Dressing in the same style of clothing as their ancestors did in Poland in the 1700s, Chasidic Jews observe traditional rules of modest dress and their own particular customs. Women and young girls cover their arms and legs, while making sure not to wear clothes that would be considered male clothing (they wear skirts or dresses). Men often wear dark suits and fur hats. Some of the specific details of their clothing vary from community to community and identify Chasidic Jews as followers of one group or another. The way they dress may look unusual to us, but it is simply part of their unique expression of Judaism.

Is every synagogue the same?

There are many different Jewish communities in our world. Just as the people who worship, study, and meet in these synagogues differ from one another, so too do synagogues have their own special ways of being designed and used. Some synagogues have pools and basketball courts and catering halls, and some may be just one room. One thing that all synagogues have in common though is a sanctuary, a space for prayer, study, and meditation.

Some synagogues are lavish buildings with stained-glassed windows and vaulted ceilings. The holy ark in the sanctuary may contain several Torahs, each one dressed in beautiful, jeweled coverings with silver ornaments dangling around the scrolls. These synagogues are places that might inspire a person to whisper when walking inside. They are designed to make a worshiper feel humble in God's presence. Other synagogues have sanctuaries that feel like a person's living room. They are cozy, with movable seats. The ark containing the Torah may be moved easily from one location to another. Rather than being awe-inspiring structures, these synagogues feel more like a comfortable, homey space.

The sanctuaries in many synagogues are designed so that the person praying faces east, toward Jerusalem. Synagogues built in the Ashkenazic tradition of Eastern Europe have a lectern or table in front of the ark where the rabbi and cantor and service leaders stand.

The service leader faces the congregation. Sephardic synagogues have a lectern for the service leader in the middle of the rows of seats. Instead of standing in front of the people praying, the service leader is next to the other people in the congregation. Orthodox synagogues often have a divider, called a *m'chitzah*, separating sections for men and women. Traditionally, men and women did not sit together during worship because it was considered too distracting. Some synagogues have a women's gallery on a second floor.

The next time you are on vacation in a different city or country, try to visit a local synagogue and see how different or similar it is to your synagogue at home.

In spite of differences in the design of synagogues, Jews are taught to behave in certain ways in a synagogue. We show respect during religious services, do not enter and leave constantly, do not bring food or drinks into the sanctuary, do not speak during certain parts of the *Amidah* section of worship (the central portion of the prayer service), and cover our heads if this is the custom of the community. The way a synagogue looks inside teaches us a great deal about the people who pray and meet inside of it.

Resources for Further Reading on Jewish Diversity

BOOKS FOR ADULTS

Choices in Modern Jewish Thought: A Partisan Guide, 2nd ed., by Eugene Borowitz. Behrman House Publishing, 1995.

Conservative Judaism: The New Century, by Neil Gillman, Behrman House Publishing, 1993.

A Guide to Jewish Religious Practice, by Isaac Klein. The Jewish Theological Seminary of America, 1992.

Jewish Living: A Guide to Contemporary Reform Practice, by Mark Washofsky. UAHC Press, 2001.

One People, Two Worlds: A Reform Rabbi and an Orthodox Rabbi Explore the Issues That Divide Them, by Ammiel Hirsch and Yosef Reinman. Schocken Books, 2003.

BOOKS FOR CHILDREN

The Atlas of Great Jewish Communities, by Sondra Leiman. UAHC Press, 2002.

A Child's First Book of Jewish Holidays, by Alfred J. Kolatch. Jonathan David Publishers, 1997.

The Jewish Child's First Book of Why, by Alfred J. Kolatch. Jonathan David Publishers, 1992.

The Jewish Kids Catalog, by Chaya Burstein. Jewish Publication Society, 1983.

Appendix

A Brief History of the Arab-Jewish Conflict

Like the Jews, some Arabs have lived in Israel for many, many years. When more and more Jewish people started to move back to Israel and buy land in the last part of the 1800s, some of the Arabs living there attacked the new Jewish settlers. In 1917, when Great Britain took control of Israel, then known by the name given to it by the Romans as Palestine, the British promised that the Jews could have a homeland there. But they also promised the Arabs that they could have the land. In 1922, Arabs were given land in what is now the country of Jordan. But many Arabs still lived in Israel. In 1947, the United Nations created a plan to divide the land so that there could be both a Jewish state and an Arab state. The Jews agreed to this "Partition Plan." The Arabs did not agree and said that they would declare war as soon as Israel became an independent state.

In 1948, the United Nations voted to create a Jewish state for the five-hundred thousand Jews living there. David Ben-Gurion became the first prime minister of the modern State of Israel, and Chaim

Weizmann was elected to be the first president. The morning after the vote, Israel was invaded by its Arab neighbors. The Israeli War of Independence lasted more than a year. Nonetheless, Jews continued to come live in the new State of Israel. Many of these new Jewish immigrants had nowhere else to go, because their homes, their jobs, and their families had been taken away from them during the Holocaust in Europe. Some of these new immigrants came from Arab countries like Morocco, Yemen, and Iraq, where their lives were in danger simply because they were Jewish. The Jews needed their homeland, Israel, where they could live safely in freedom.

There have been many wars since Israel declared independence in 1948. In 1967, the Six-Day War took place. Though Israel's Arab neighbors on all sides were trying to "exterminate the State of Israel for all time," in those six short days, Israel held off its attackers and gained control over some of the land that had belonged to the Arab countries around it. The people who lived in those areas taken over by Israel in 1967 are known as Palestinians, from the word "Palestine." In 1973, on Yom Kippur, Egypt and Syria attacked Israel. Although Israel was expecting some kind of attack, the timing of it on Yom Kipur came as a surprise. But Israel fought back and survived. For many years, there have continued to be problems with countries to Israel's north, Lebanon and Syria.

Israel has tried hard to make peace with its neighbors. In 1979, representatives from Israel and Egypt, with the help of the United States, were able to sign a peace treaty between their countries. In 1991, Israelis met with Arab neighbors from Syria, Lebanon, Jordan, and the Palestinians to talk about peace. More recently, in 1993, Palestinian chairman Yasir Arafat and Israel's prime minister, Yitzhak Rabin, met to work toward making peace. Arafat, Rabin, and Israeli foreign minister Shimon Peres were awarded the Nobel Peace

Prize in 1994 for their efforts to make peace between the Palestinians and the Israelis. A peace agreement with Jordan was signed in 1994. In 1999 and 2000, Israel's prime minister, Ehud Barak, met with Chairman Arafat yet again to try to work out a peace agreement, with the help of the American president, Bill Clinton.

In the summer of 2005, under the leadership of Israeli prime minister Ariel Sharon, Israel undertook a process of "disengagement" from the Gaza Strip. All Jewish settlements were emptied, and the area came completely under control of the Palestinan Authority. At the time of this writing, the United States is again involved in helping Israel and the Palestinians create a lasting, workable peace.

Glossary

Aliyah: Hebrew word meaning "going up." Refers to the honor of reciting the blessings before and after reading the Torah in synagogue. Also means moving to Israel.

Ashkenazic: Jews whose families come from Eastern Europe; or practices that reflect the customs of Jews from that part of the world.

bar mitzvah: From the Aramaic and Hebrew words that literally mean "son of the commandment." When a Jewish boy reaches the age of thirteen years old, he is considered to be a bar mitzvah, a person who is considered old enough to fulfill many of the commandments. Often refers to the Shabbat service led by a young man when he reaches the age of thirteen and the celebration associated with this milestone.

bat mitzvah: Hebrew words that literally mean "daughter of the commandment." When a Jewish girl reaches the age of thirteen years old (in some communities, twelve), she is considered to be a bat mitzvah, a person who is old enough to fulfill many of the commandments. Often refers to the Shabbat service led by a young woman when she reaches this age and the celebration associated with this milestone.

chalutz (plural, ***chalutzim***): Hebrew word that means "pioneer." Refers to the immigrants to the Land of Israel or Palestine during the 1800s and early 1900s who purchased and farmed the land and established communities.

chazan: Hebrew word meaning "cantor." Refers to a cantor who is a man.

chazanit: Hebrew word referring to a female cantor.

chesed: Hebrew word for "kindness" and "gracious act."

chuppah: A canopy held up by four poles under which the bride and groom stand during a Jewish wedding ceremony. It symbolizes the home of the couple.

d'var Torah: Literally, "word of Torah." A short speech typically delivered before or after the reading of a section of Torah to highlight major themes in the reading.

Eretz Yisrael: Hebrew for "Land of Israel."

haftarah: The haftarah portion is the reading from the part of the Bible known as the Prophets. This reading repeats a theme from the Torah portion that is read on Shabbat. These readings tell about how important God is in Jewish history. Each week there is a different Torah portion and matching haftarah portion.

Haggadah: Hebrew word meaning "telling." Refers to the book used to tell the story of the Jews' Exodus from Egypt. This book is used at the Passover seder.

halachah: Hebrew word meaning "the way." Refers to traditional Jewish laws.

holy ark: The specially designed closet or container holding the Torah scrolls in a synagogue. In Hebrew, known as *aron kodesh*.

Kaddish: Prayer that appears in various parts of the prayer service and marks divisions in the sections of the service. Traditionally this prayer is recited by a mourner for eleven months following the death of a close relative. The prayer is actually written in the language of Aramaic and does not refer to death at all, but discusses the holiness of God and life.

ketubah: Hebrew word for a Jewish wedding contract that spells out the rights and responsibilities of the couple.

Kiddush: Hebrew word meaning "sanctification" or "holy." Refers to the special blessings chanted or recited over wine or grape juice on Shabbat and the Festivals.

kippah: Hebrew word meaning "head covering." Refers to the skullcap worn by Jewish men when they pray. Some Jewish women wear a *kippah* when they are praying. Some Jewish people wear a *kippah* almost all the time to show that God is above them. Also called a yarmulke.

K'lal Yisrael: Hebrew expression meaning "the peoplehood of Israel." It means that everyone who is Jewish is connected. All Jews are part of the same extended family.

kosher: Hebrew word meaning "ritually fit." Usually refers to the way a food is prepared or whether or not that food is considered to meet with Jewish dietary laws. Can also refer to the condition of a Torah, tallit, or other important Jewish ritual object.

Ladino: A language that was spoken by Sephardic Jews from Western Europe. It is a bit of a mix of Spanish and Hebrew. It is still spoken in some homes today.

m'chitzah: Hebrew word meaning "divider." Refers to the divider separating seating sections for men and women in traditional synagogues.

menorah: Hebrew word meaning "lamp." A seven-branched menorah is the symbol of the State of Israel. The menorah is mentioned in the Torah as part of the ancient Temple. An eight-branched menorah lit for the festival of Chanukah is known as a *chanukiyah*.

mensch: Yiddish word meaning "man" or "human being." Being a mensch means being a human being and acting in the best and kindest way possible.

mezuzah: Hebrew word meaning "doorpost." Refers to the ceremonial object on a doorpost that contains the *Sh'ma* and *V'ahavta* prayers found originally in the Book of Deuteronomy in the Torah.

midrash: From the Hebrew root meaning "to explain." A story that fills in a gap or explains something from a part of the Bible. Between the years 300 and 1000 C.E., many midrashim (plural) were written and collected in Palestine.

mikveh: Hebrew word meaning "ritual bath." Refers to the special pool that is used for dipping when people convert to Judaism and for other important times in Jewish people's lives.

minyan: Hebrew word meaning "quorum" or minimum number of people necessary to meet in order to say certain prayers. Ten people over the age of bar or bat mitzvah are required for a minyan.

Mishnah: The collection of Jewish laws arranged according to six major categories, or "orders." Based on laws that were passed down orally, the Mishnah was written in Hebrew and was edited in Palestine at the end of the second century C.E. by Rabbi Judah HaNasi.

mitzvah (plural, **mitzvot**): Hebrew word for "commandment." According to the Rabbis, there are 613 mitzvot found in the Torah. Sometimes used colloquially to mean "good deed."

seder: Hebrew word for "order." Refers to the special dinner at the beginning of Passover during which the story of the Jews' Exodus from Egypt is told. The different parts of the dinner and the telling of the story take place in a very specific order.

sephardic: Jews whose families come from Western Europe; or practices that reflect the customs of Jews from that part of the world.

shalom: Hebrew word for "peace," "hello," and "goodbye." It connotes wholeness or completion.

shivah: Hebrew word referring to the seven days following a loved one's funeral that close relatives take to mourn for a loved one who has died.

Shoah: Hebrew word referring to the Holocaust. It means "complete destruction by fire."

Shulchan Aruch: Literally means "Set Table." Refers to an important code of Jewish law written for Sephardic Jews by Joseph Caro of Safed, Israel (1488–1575), printed in Venice in 1565, and interpreted by Rabbi Moses Isserles (1530–1572) for Ashkenazic Jews.

tallit: Hebrew word for a prayer shawl worn during morning prayers and on the eve of Yom Kippur. Often referred to as a "tallis" in Yiddish. The fringes on the ends signify the commandments.

tallit kattan: Hebrew term for a long piece of cloth with fringes on its corners worn under clothes. It is *katan*, or small, compared to the large prayer shawl (a tallit) worn over someone's clothes while praying.

Talmud: Jewish law and stories that were written down in Babylonia between the second and fifth centuries and in Jerusalem between the second and fourth centuries. The Talmud is made up of the Mishnah (essentially six areas of law, written in Hebrew) and the Gemara (commentary by the Rabbis on the Mishnah, written in Aramaic).

Tanach: Hebrew word for "Bible," taken from the first letters of the three different parts of the Bible: *Torah*; *N'vi-im*, *K'tuvim*. Refers to the thirty-nine books of the Hebrew Bible and includes the

Torah (the five Books of Moses), *N'vi-im* (the Prophets), and *K'tuvim* (the Writings).

Ten Commandments: Also known as the Decalogue, from the Greek meaning "ten words." These ten rules form the basis of a system of behavior of Jewish law in the Torah. They appear in two different places in the Torah, Exodus 20 and Deuteronomy 5. There are slight differences between the two sets of commandments, and some writers and churches divide the commandments a bit differently. Generally, the commandments are interpreted as follows:

1. I the Eternal am your God who brought you out of the land of Egypt, the house of bondage.
2. You shall have no other gods beside Me. You shall not make for yourself a sculptured image, or any likeness of what is in the heavens above, or on the earth below, or in the waters under the earth. You shall not bow down to them or serve them. For I the Eternal your God am an impassioned God, visiting the guilt of the parents upon the children, upon the third and upon the fourth generations of those who reject Me, but showing kindness to the thousandth generation of those who love Me and keep My commandments.
3. You shall not swear falsely by the name of the Eternal your God; for the Eternal will not clear one who swears falsely by God's name.
4. Remember the Sabbath day and keep it holy. Six days you shall labor and do all your work, but the seventh day is a Sabbath of the Eternal your God: you shall not do any work—you, your son or daughter, your male or female slave, or your cattle, or the stranger who is within your settlements. For in six days the Eternal made heaven and earth and sea—

and all that is in them—and then rested on the seventh day; therefore the Eternal blessed the Sabbath day and hallowed it.

5. Honor your father and your mother, that you may long endure on the land that the Eternal your God is assigning to you.

6. You shall not murder.

7. You shall not commit adultery.

8. You shall not steal.

9. You shall not bear false witness against your neighbor.

10. You shall not covet your neighbor's house: you shall not covet your neighbor's wife, nor male or female slave, nor ox nor ass, nor anything that is your neighbor's.

tikkun olam: Hebrew phrase for "repairing the world." Jews are supposed to work to fix our planet through our actions.

tzedakah: Hebrew word meaning "righteousness" or "righteous giving." *Tzedakah* means justice or fixing what is wrong in the world and making things fair through our help and giving.

tz'niut: Hebrew word meaning "modesty." Refers to acting and dressing in ways that show humility and modesty before others and God. Different Jewish communities have different standards of *tz'niut*.

yetzer hara: Hebrew phrase referring to the bad or evil impulse human beings possess. This inclination or impulse does battle with a conflicting impulse for good (*yetzer hatov*).

yetzer hatov: Hebrew phrase referring to the good impulse human beings possess. This inclination or impulse does battle with a conflicting impulse for evil (*yetzer hara*).

Yiddish: A language that was very commonly spoken by Jews in Eastern Europe. It is still spoken today. The language sounds like a mix of German and Hebrew.